HOME WINE MAKING
—all the Year Round

HOME WINE MAKING
—all the Year Round

H. E. BRAVERY

MACDONALD · LONDON

First published in 1966
  by Max Parrish and Co Ltd

Reissued in 1968 by
  Macdonald and Co. (Publishers) Ltd,
  St Giles House,
  49 Poland Street, London W.1

This impression 1972

SBN 356 01129 1

Reproduced and printed in Great Britain by
Redwood Press Limited, Trowbridge & London

Contents

Foreword

This book is entirely different from other books of mine on this subject – though, of course, I have again covered the causes of spoiled wine and how to avoid them. I have also to cover again certain factual information and describe the best utensils to use. These details are essential in a work of this sort if it is to be of a ha'porth of use.

There are several reasons for preparing this book, the main being that very soon there will be none of the ingredients for wines that today we take for granted. Indeed, in a great many areas, the wild ingredient has gone altogether.

Let me give you a single example and you will be able to pin-point a hundred more.

Years ago my brothers and sisters and I used to go into the fields surrounding our old house and gather, in quite a short time, great basketfuls of dandelions, cowslips, elderflowers, blackberries, sloes, elderberries and wild strawberries from which our parents made heaven knows how many gallons of wine each year. We also had an orchard and a large fruit-garden which yielded umpteen gallons of wine each year – my parents were very fond of their home-made wines.

I can recall the massive tubs with their great foaming heads and I remember we used to dip a cup into these, drink a little of the still fermenting wine and then totter about the orchard pretending we were tight. I myself made many hundreds of gallons from fruits from the fields and hedgerows of that area prior to moving away.

When we look to those same fields for our ingredients today, all we see is a jungle of brickwork. The new estates must be built, the new factories and by-passes put in, and as these come, so our ingredients vanish. Soon, there will be very little wild ingredients left for the picking except in a few remote areas where the great god 'commerce' might never cast his covetous glances.

Gardens which at one time were big enough to keep a family of six or more in fruits and vegetables the whole year round, are getting smaller and smaller. So, soon, besides the wild ingredient being in very short supply, the garden will not produce a quarter of the need of the average wine-maker.

But loss of wild and garden ingredients is not the only reason for preparing a book dealing in making wines without them. Other factors must be considered.

Fruits bought from the greengrocer used to be a lot cheaper than they are today and were often quite suitable for wine-making. Today, however, it is a different story. Plums, damsons and similar fruits are brought into the shops while under-ripe and are intended mainly for jam-making. These under-ripe fruit are not suitable wine ingredients because, being under-ripe, they contain too much acid. Black and red-currants appear these days in little square baskets containing enough to make one bottle of wine and the cost is about three shillings – prohibitive. Imported grapes and other imported fruits, with perhaps the exception of oranges, are also much too expensive if it is to be profitable to make wine. Peaches and apricots are also very expensive and are usually under-ripe when purchased. So the greengrocer, like the countryside, is no longer what it used to be.

Another important factor is the trend – or should I say need – for more and more people to live in flats and smaller modern houses, means that cellar, the outhouse, the semi-basement, or the scullery or wash-house in which most people used to make their wines will soon be no more. With all these things soon to be gone, one might well ask how on earth is anybody going to be able to make wines at all. Wine-makers are immensely resourceful. Once having made good wines, as everybody making them does these days, they are unlikely to be put off by a few obstacles. Indeed, many thousands already make wines in small houses and flats in cities and large towns where wild ingredients are seen only from trains on the way home from the office or factory. These people are still using what little wild or garden ingredients they can find. These wine-makers and many thousands more will make wines in modern accommodations using the modern ingredients now available while following the simple recipes and directions here. Modern ingredients and modern methods make it possible for quite useful amounts of wine to be made in a very small place. I have only a quarter of the space I was once accustomed to and although I am lucky enough to have a little wild and garden stuff, I make quite large amounts of top-quality wines each year from the modern ingredient. These allow us to make really remarkable wines with the minimum labour, space and cash outlay. So, we have here the first wine-making book of the future which will be invaluable to those wishing to make top-quality wines today.

Introduction

Necessity (so they say), is the mother of invention. Be that as it may, I do not think it has been invention but rather a gradual realisation of a coming need, and the passing over from one type of wine-making to another. That necessity comes into it there is no doubt.

Here we are – most of us – faced with the problem of finding ever-dwindling ingredients or being more resourceful in using specially prepared stuffs for making fine wines. In the first place the gradual passing over from one type of ingredient to another is a good thing for it allowed those with experience to use that experience to evolve simple methods and recipes for using the new type of ingredient. The fact that we can make Vermouth and wines flavoured with world famous liqueurs easily and cheaply is the outcome.

Also the outcome is a new kind of simple, trouble-free wine-making. No longer have we to go miles in search of scarce ingredients, but merely open a tin, jar or bottle and away we go.

But do not imagine this kind of wine-making does not give such good results as when fresh fruits are used. Modern ingredients make top-quality wines that win prizes for the few people already using them. The simple fact is that this book will enable wine-makers to keep in step with progress. Naturally, there is a die-hard core fighting to stay in the past. No one can blame them for that because they are fortunate enough to live near wild ingredients from which the traditional home-made wines are made.

But we who find our once abundant ingredients in short supply must either move with the times or give up wine-making – heaven forbid. So no one need give up wine-making – that is clear. Indeed, many thousands still making wines by traditional methods and with traditional ingredients and who find the labour of collecting them a bit irksome in these fast-moving times, will be aroused to new and greater interest when they see how easy modern ingredients are to use. Those who are about to take up wine-making for the first time will never know how much they owe to the modern ingredient. Having been making wines for over a quarter century, I naturally found the change-over simplicity itself. Nevertheless, the past few years have been spent in innumerable trials and experiments with every sort of new ingredients in order to find simple methods and recipes to produce top-quality wines quickly and cheaply – wines capable of holding their own with commercial products costing ten times as much.

In chapter 20 it will be found that we employ bananas with other ingredients: roots, dried fruits and so on. These are not new ingredients, of course, but the recipes are and the wines made from them really are excellent. The bother, if it can be called that, is that we cannot liken them to commercial products as we can say that elderberries will make a Burgundy or port style and blackberries an excellent imitation of Beaujolais. Nevertheless, top-rate wine they do make.

As mentioned, I have been experimenting for years with these and countless other sorts of ingredients, and I am now able to pass on the results of these years of work confident that my readers will enjoy equal success.

I

Points to Ponder

Make no mistake about this, all recipes in this book make top-rate wines, but this does not mean that you will like them all. This is owing to the simple fact that all tastes are not the same. Some like sweet wines, others like them dry, others like them medium sweet to medium dry. Some like light wines, others like them medium light to medium heavy or heavy like the better class ports . . .

It is the same with beers. Some like the light lager types, while others like light or brown ales or stouts or mild draught beers or bitter. And no one can decide without trial which they are going to like best of all. Yet all these wines and beers are first-class products.

And so it is with making wines: you will have to choose from several makings which you prefer and then concentrate on these, making others in experimental lots in order to find a wide variety to suit your individual tastes. Middle Eastern rulers have the right idea; they not only have a variety of wines but also a variety of wives to suit their mood or fancy, and what's more, they have both the wine and the wife of their fancy at the same time. I must have been born on the wrong side of the Mediterranean!

Choosing the recipe that is going to make the wine most likely to suit you is easy if you use those in chapter 16, calling for the use of T'Noirot extracts, as one has only to see the name of the extract to find the type of wine that will result. But in many other cases it is not possible to liken the finished wine to a commercial product; this may be because I have not tasted all the commercial wines on the market, some of those I have tasted I would not wish to imitate because in my opinion, they are fit only for use as weed-killers. Some are so flavourless and so acid as to be quite unpalatable, yet to many people these very wines are perfectly delightful.

It is a fact that when using blackberries and elderberries and other wild and garden fruits we are able to imitate well-known and very popular commercial wines, but this is not necessarily the case here unless, as I have already mentioned, you are using T'Noirot extracts. Nevertheless, very attractive wines are made from the other recipes in this book.

2

Wine-making, Then and Now

This is not intended to be a history of amateur wine-making, but as a wine-maker of over twenty-five years practical experience, and a number of years in beer making (though I ought not to mention this because until April 1963 I was breaking the law), I do feel that wine-makers of to-day who enjoy using simple methods and recipes with top-class results assured should know something of the work that has been necessary in their evolution.

Twenty years ago home-made wines were poor indeed compared with those made today. Modern methods are the results of work by questing thinkers who were not satisfied as our forebears were to shrug off failures as just one of those things.

My grandparents made vast amounts of wines, beers and ciders. My parents did likewise. Both became famous in their localities for the beverages they made. Some were good according to the tastes, standards and requirements of the average wine-drinker of the times, but none of them would be able to stand on their own feet today, any more than could any local who had taken more than two pints of grandfather's beer or cider.

17

No one could understand how he made them so strong. Probably he himself had no notion. Most likely it had occurred to him that if 'so much' sugar made a good wine it should also make good beers. This it did, if only in making them as strong as wines. As everybody knows, drinking wine by the pint is likely to unsteady anybody.

Despite the reputation they enjoyed, like countless others up and down their country, they had their failures. Naturally, they never told of them. The fact that they made so many good lots is remarkable when one considers in the light of our present-day knowledge of the subject, that they were using the very methods that brought failures more often than success.

The normal practice was to gather the fruit and crush it; add water and sugar without boiling either and, without adding yeast, merely let it ferment by any yeast that was on the fruits or floating about in the air. Flowers were treated in the same fashion. No wonder they had so many failures. By failures I do not mean those over acid, often insipid, muddy-looking concoctions accepted as wines by those who knew no better. These were merely disappointing lots to be used up when no one was around to see them; the better being kept for when someone worth impressing turned up – which was often.

I can recall vividly those great tubs of forty gallons and more – of wines and beers with their foaming heads alive with wasps and flies crawling all over them.

No one thought of covering the vessels to guard against dust from beaten carpets and sifted ashes. Everything blew through the winery. And the converted pigsty in which my grandfather, and later my father, brewed their famed beers, was equally unhygienic. This state of affairs was common-place, they accepted this.

When often I had to run errands for the 'gentry' living in the 'big houses' in the area (not having been born with a silver spoon in my mouth) I used to see wines and beers being made under similar conditions – any barn or outhouse being suitable. Being about eight or nine years old at the time all I knew of wines and beers was that they made some people sing and others fight. But wines were made long before this. They were made before Noah – that is if you can believe that story of the Ark without having taken a drink or two first.

Indeed, they were made by the most primitive of man. One reads in accounts by early explorers of concoctions made by natives chewing herbs, nuts or other materials and spitting the 'cud' into a vessel which later became the fermentation vessel. All members of the tribe are said to have taken turns at chewing and spitting until the vessel contained sufficient material. It was then fermented by whatever yeast happened to come along.

It is noted that explorers and early travellers spoke highly of the concoctions turned out in this fashion – probably before they had seen how they were made. One often reads of the delightful wine-like drinks turned out by such and such tribe: 'a delightful beverage when indulged in makes one merry'. I imagine many of the so-called 'love-potions' were little more than crude alcohol produced in similar fashion. After all, all of us – or should I speak for myself only – are a little less inhibited when we have had a drink or two. Dusky maidens knowing this tempted shy young warriors with a half coconut shell of this stuff and most likely took a little herself to help things along. Having made them less inhibited it was easy to persuade the young bloods to make love. Thus this special love-potion was nothing more than a drop of spittoon wine. Personally, having seen some really lovely dusky maidens I am at a loss to understand the need for love potions . . . !

Wines – if you can call them that – are still being made by natives today. And alas, as my considerable mail proves, people in this country, Canada, U.S.A., Australia, New Zealand, indeed, the world over are still following the antiquated methods as used by my grandparents. This is understandable up to a point because these methods are those taken to these countries by the pioneers.

There are still countless thousands not yet acquainted with the few scientific details and scraps of equipment needed to transform their wines into something worth having.

Naturally, my early efforts were made by the same methods as used by my grandparents because these were the only known methods. But I was not content: there must be a reason for all the disappointments and failures, I told myself, otherwise how could the trade turn out such wonderful stuff.

The trade was unlikely to give much help to those striving to find the secrets. There were no books on the subject other than collections of recipes to be used with the very methods already described. Even the immortal Mrs Beeton who was supposed to know everything could not give a clue. Not being a chemist and not realising that there might be a chemical aspect to the subject, I continued making them in this antiquated fashion always striving to find out the reason for those nagging faults – vinegariness, over-acidity, cloudiness and all the other faults that were to mar almost all our efforts.

Encyclopaedias were studied for hours – nay, days – even weeks. Clue upon clue studied, possibilities considered. But encyclopaedias do not normally cover subjects fully enough, so I and those helping me felt we were still battering our heads against a wall.

And then, quite by chance, we discovered some useful information about yeasts, the various sorts, their uses and their effects. First we learned that some yeasts were suitable for making wines while others floating about in the air were capable of ruining the stuff. At last we were to understand that most of the causes of disappointment and failures were due to 'unwanted' or 'undesirable' yeasts. And the fact that these were on the very fruits we were making wines with was a great thrill indeed. For here was the root cause of disaster – contained in the very ingredients.

Boil to destroy was the obvious answer and we worked accordingly, destroying the yeast on the fruits and adding fresh yeast when the must had cooled. But our wines, while better in flavour and body, were almost always very cloudy. Popular clarifiers like isinglass and geletine only worsened matters.

Some cleared to brilliance without the use of clarifiers. This deepened the mystery; why should some clear in this fashion and others refuse to clear even when 'clarified' with clarifiers. After a long time we learned something about pectin and how this is boiled into fruit juices, preventing wines from clearing. But we had to boil to destroy unwanted yeast, didn't we? It seemed at this stage that there was no method for making clear wines.

We continued to experiment, learning as we went along more about yeasts and bacteria, and we discovered how to destroy the unwanted yeasts and the bacteria on fruits without boiling them. We tried this; the result was brilliantly-clear wines with a better flavour, more body and bouquet. The wonderful stuff that made all this possible is known as sodium metabisulphite and is now available in tablet form known as Campden fruit-preserving tablets.

That we had discovered nothing new to the science of wine-making did not dishearten us. For we were, I am sure, the first group of people to employ this chemical in wine-making – that is, outside the trade. Thus we are able to take credit for introducing this type of wine-making in the first real practical book on wine-making: *Home Wine-making Without Failures*, Vol. I.

Having discovered the method that has now become so popular throughout the world, I still had no real answer to the problem of good wines being spoiled on keeping. Good wines that cleared to brilliance, had top-rate flavour, excellent bouquet and fair alcohol content, were now easy to make, but they often spoilt on keeping. Yeast and bacteria are in the air; therefore they must be inside the very bottles we fill and on the corks we use to close them. So, to prevent our top-class wines spoiling we had not only to sterilise bottles and corks, but also keep air away from them during all stages of production: for in the very air we breath was death to our wines. Campden solution sterilised bottles; corks had to be boiled whether it harmed them or not. Today we have plastic corks which last a lifetime and are sterilised with Campden solution.

And so we were another stage nearer complete success. The final link in this mysterious chain came with the introduction of what I have often described as the best friend wine-makers will ever have – the fermentation lock. This little bit of twisted glass tubing forms the mighty 'wall of China' behind which our wines are safe from attack from outside.

Not only does this prevent spoilage yeasts and bacteria reaching the wines, but it assists in increasing the alcohol content which means that wines are preserved by the amount of alcohol present. And so we had – after many many years of work – discovered secrets withheld from us. I say this because commercial producers had been using these methods with their grape juices all along.

So now we knew all we needed to do in order to make top-rate wines that cleared to brilliance of their own accord and which kept well.

From this stage it has been only a story of progress. And it is somewhat ironical that after struggling for years in the dark, once we had brought daylight into our activities, the chief chemist of a famous British winery, who knew it all years before us, became interested and put a lot of useful information at our disposal. Helpful as he was, and grateful as we are to him, he did not give nearly as much information as he might have done, which, of course, was understandable.

Learning as we did taught us more than any chemical encyclopaedia or anybody could have taught us in talks or lectures. After all, it is all very well to know what to do, but knowledge is useless without practical experience and learning the hard way is surely the most thorough training.

But our quest for perfection did not end here. In these changing times, tastes were also changing: most of us returning from the war had tasted some of the many foreign wines and I for one, decided that it would be quite something if we could imitate them.

We had learned over our years of training that the grape forms the only 'true' medium for making genuine wines. Any wine made from other materials was not wine in the strict meaning of the word, but was merely an imitation. The fact that they were excellent makes no difference. This, in my view is bunkum – but there it is.

It is a fact that the grape is the best medium for fermentation. This is because it contains all the necessary elements of a thorough fermentation which wines of inferior quality lack; and what is more, they usually contain these elements in the best proportions. Therefore, if we were to imitate commercially-produced wines we had, in so far as we could, to introduce into our musts the chemical matter contained in grapes. Many English fruits do contain these elements in small quantities, so we had to make adjustments in some cases, and where, for example, we used potatoes and other roots or grains such as wheat which contained none of the elements contained in grapes, we had to make wide and varied adjustments before we could hope to produce a must bearing any resemblance at all to the composition of a must prepared from grapes.

Tannin, acids, sugar content – all had to be balanced to a certain extent and the recipe evolved later after many trials. But we were still a long way from our goal.

All kinds of fruit were tried, various methods, too, but always there was something lacking. For one thing we were not obtaining the fuller flavours, the bouquet we needed, nor that illusive vinous odour that makes for a quality wines. For it was real quality that we were seeking now, but we had only baker's yeast to work with.

Then came wine yeasts. By this time, there was actually a firm marketing them, unknown to us. These we tried at once with the Campden solution method already mentioned and the result was quality, quality all the way. But the story does not end there. Different yeasts gave different results with different fruit. So we had to find the yeast most suitable for the type of wine we wanted to make from the variety of fruits we were using. More years of work were necessary before we were at last satisfied that we could set out to make a certain type of wine similar to a commercial product using English fruits in certain proportions and get the wine-type we wanted. But when we could say before we began 'this will be a good imitation of Beaujolais – or Burgundy or sauternes', or whatever it was we were imitating, and then find it was as near to our goal as anyone is likely to get, we had, I think, reached our zenith. But I was wrong. We are still learning about this subject just as science is learning about space.

And so we have progressed from our primitive methods where failures were more likely than success to modern methods where success is assured. During all these years others were working on different lines to myself and my friends. Many people liked the flavours of wines made by the boiling method which produced those cloudy wines. Clarifying them was a problem they had to overcome, and they did this with the use of an enzyme which destroys the pectin in the fruits, thus preventing it holding minute solids in suspension to cloud the finished product. Starch-destroying enzymes are now also employed where starch-bearing ingredients such as roots and grains are used.

So now we may use whichever method makes the kind of wine desired without fuss or bother and with a minimum of labour and time.

Continental holidays are teaching many people to appreciate wines, and the habit of taking them with meals is catching on over here to such an extent that many wine-makers make all the wines normally used with a meal, and what is more, they are preferred to the commercially produced wines of the very parts of the continent they visited. Surely no greater evidence is needed to prove just how far we have advanced from the days of not so long ago.

But to make these wines also called for years of experimentation, for we were using English fruits instead of the grape of the area whose wine we were imitating. To have succeeded is no mean achievement. But here, there is a small element of gloom.

For during all these years, there was an absolute super-abundance of garden and wild fruits available, and it was these fruits that made such wonderful wines.

Alas, this is not so today. Gardens are smaller, the vast areas of open country that produced such an abundance of fruits, blackberries, elderberries, sloes, crab-apples and the flowers commonly used for wines are quickly vanishing under new estates and roads. And the practice of farmers and local-authorities using weed-killers and insecticides so indiscriminately is rendering much of what remains unsafe to use.

So it would seem that many years of work had gone to waste merely because we had perfected the means of making quality wines with ingredients that were to become almost extinct. There are still some about, of course, but the ever-growing army of wine-makers are after them, so they are difficult to find unless you happen to get there first. I live in an area that once abounded in all the requirements of an ardent wine-maker. There is only a quarter of the area where wild fruit still grow, and it is now common to see some fifty people trying to gather enough for a couple of gallons, when only a few short years ago my friends and I were the only ones to gather them. And if the present threat to take the new A25 road through the area materialises there will be hardly enough fruits left to make it worth-while collecting them.

That this state of affairs would arise eventually was foreseen by some of us, so that we decided not to be caught unawares.

By this time, concentrated grape juices had become available as had the synthetic must, dried fruit that normally grow wild, fruit pulps, extracts and other materials. And, although we were loath to admit that we would have to find other means of making wines leaving behind us the ingredients that had given us such wonderful wines and immense pleasure, we realised that these once-scoffed-at ingredients would have to play an enormous part in future wine-making.

So we had to experiment again, gradually getting the hang of understanding the different techniques necessary to make good wines by simple, fool-proof methods using hitherto almost unknown ingredients. What can only be described as our vast experience helped us enormously so that we quickly evolved recipes for using the new ingredients with methods that anybody could follow.

The results are contained in this book, and I am sure those following directions will be in for a lifetime of simple trouble-free wine-making with the very best results assured.

From the foregoing it will be seen that modern wine-making is not something that just happened, but is the result of years of painstaking work by a dedicated few.

3

Yeast Fermentation

Without yeast our fruit juice and water mixtures – musts – would remain musts. It is the yeast we add that makes the wine for us. Yeast feeds upon the sugar turning half into alcohol and half into carbon-dioxide gas – the gas we see leaving the wine during fermentation.

The action of yeast has been very fully detailed in a previous work, so I cannot give the fullest details here. Nevertheless, I can explain that as soon as yeast is added to a must it begins to reproduce itself, living on the sugar to sustain and nourish each of the millions of new generations that are formed. In doing this it produces as a by-product, the all important alcohol we seek. This it continues to do until about 14-15% of alcohol by volume is produced. At this stage the yeast is destroyed by the alcohol so that no more is made. At this point also fermentation ceases and nothing will induce it to start again, not even fresh yeast because this would be killed instantly by the alcohol already in the wine.

To produce the amount of alcohol just mentioned

29

the yeast needs two and a half pounds of sugar per gallon of must. Any sugar in excess of this amount will be left unfermented to sweeten the wine.

If you will take a look at the table in the section 'Sweet or Dry' you will see precisely what I mean.

In the old days – and I am sorry to say, even to-day – baker's yeast was all anybody used to make wines. Some did, and I confess that I did, make some passable wines with it. But since wine yeasts have come our way in recent years, baker's yeast has in all but remote areas been completely ousted. Wines made with baker's yeast cannot be compared with those made with wine yeast. These yeasts not only ensure a brilliant wine but they also improve greatly the flavour, bouquet, alcohol content and keeping qualities.

The secret of success in modern times is to use a good wine yeast with a fermentation lock and a modern method. If you do this your wines will not only be ten times better than you could hope to make with baker's yeast and no fermentation lock, but they will be comparable with the best commercial products and will keep well; and what is more, improve with age.

When to add the yeast is given in the various methods. The method of adding the yeast is different from baker's yeast which was merely sprinkled over the surface. Wine yeasts – which incidentally are imported from the wine-growing districts of Europe – need handling differently. The best way is to boil about half a pint of water and dissolve in this a teaspoonful of sugar. Allow this to cool and pour into a washed, sterilised and rinsed half-pint milk bottle. To this add a couple of drops of lemon juice or two or three drops P.L.J. and a teaspoonful of cold, but not stale tea. Into this pour the yeast, or stir it in if it is in dried form. Plug the neck with a firm knob of cotton wool for two days, then fit a fermentation lock. In three or four days it will be seen that this little mixture is fermenting and is ready to be added as an active yeast to a must you will have prepared. Always prepare the yeast in this manner when you know you will be ready to make the wine when the yeast in the bottle is fermenting. As soon as the must is ready, shake the yeast bottle (the starter bottle or nucleus, as it is often called), and pour about half into the mixture; the direction as to when to add this is clearly given in the methods.

The yeast remaining in the bottle may be kept alive by adding a little more boiled water and sugar, lemon juice and tea. If you do not want to keep this going, add the lot to the batch of wine – regardless of whether it was intended for one gallon or ten. Then, if you make another batch of wine while the first is still fermenting, you may take a little of the fermenting wine and add it to the new batch. If you do this shake up the wine first.

It will be seen that there is a wide variety of yeasts available. The best plan is to use an all-purpose or 'neutral' wine yeast to start with. Then, as your experience grows, use a yeast more suitable for the type of wine you are imitating. For example in some fruit wine recipes I recommend all-purpose, or perhaps a Burgundy yeast. In this case you may use the all-purpose if you wish, but because the fruit and method produces a wine of the Burgundy type, a Burgundy yeast is the better to use.

Fermentation is seen as a frothing on the surface of the must. Where fruits themselves are being fermented, these will rise to the surface to form a solid cake. Press this under the surface once a day and cover again at once.

Where no solids are present, fermentation is seen merely as a frothing, and there is nothing for you to do except follow the directions of whichever method you are using.

The important thing is to get a good fermentation. In the normal way a good fermentation comes almost naturally, but this does not mean that we cannot take special steps to ensure that we do get a really good fermentation. A good fermentation, one that is vigorous at the start, that slows down gently, and then goes on steadily until it ceases altogether makes for a better quality wine than a poor ferment that is weak throughout and ceases before the maximum alcohol is reached.

Apart from using a good yeast and a fermentation lock there are two other steps we can take. One is to use nutrient. There is nothing mysterious about these. But let me explain first the need for them. As I think everybody must know, true wines are made only from grapes. I am speaking only of true wine in the sense that only the grape can make true wine in the accepted meaning of the word 'wine'. What we do, in effect, when using ingredients other than grapes, is to make an imitation of wine – not true wine. This may sound like – and in my opinion is – nonsense. But the fact remains that, scientifically, and perhaps chemically, we do not make wines unless we use grapes. The fact that we make wines as good, and often better, than those made with grapes and carrying famous names seems to make no difference. Let me quote examples. Many people would not give you tuppence a bottle for many of the famed wines from the continent, yet they swear by their own elderberry and blackberry wines, or whichever is their favourite; and I, for that matter, do the same. Frankly, if some of my wines turned out like some of those costing 10/- and 12/- per bottle, I would promptly pour them down the sink, or invite a few people round of whom I am not particularly fond in the hope of getting rid of the wine in a slightly more dignified manner.

Yet the fact remains that the grape – and here I think is the secret, contains the elements for the best type of fermentation. So when we make wines from our less elegant materials we do not have in the must the same elements we would have if using grapes. Thus we may not get such a good fermentation.

But we can now, because nutrient salts, stimulators, nutrients, energisers or whatever they may be called amount to the same thing – yeast nutrients. These are blends of chemicals that when added to a must give it, amongst other matter, some of the chemicals it would contain if it were made up of grapes. Thus, in using nutrients as directed in the methods and recipes, we are getting nearer the basic needs of the yeast. And since it is the yeast that turns our musts into wines for us, the few extra pence spent on keeping it happy will be worth it. Another step – which is also well worth it – is to make a special fermentation cupboard.

This is detailed under its own heading. This is because beginners will not want to be bothered with this in the early stages. But having followed the recipes and having made wines better than they ever thought they could, they will want to know how to make them even better, and what is more important, how they can keep the wine warm during fermentation at practically no cost at all. The need for warmth is also explained in the heading 'Fermentation Cupboard', page 44. Having this valuable asset enables you to make wines of the best quality during winter months when wine-making is not usually a practicable proposition at all.

In the introduction to the use of T'Noirot extracts, chapter 15, I mention that the yeast needs organic matter if fermentation is to be good. There is no doubt about this. Yeast will ferment in a sugar and water solution only, but it will not ferment well simply because this alone is not the best medium for yeast production. Add nutrient matter – nutrient salts – as already mentioned and you add a certain amount of organic matter. This will not only make yeast reproduction more steady and rapid, but will shorten the fermentation period quite a lot. Add fruit pulp or other similar material such as that obtained from boiling potatoes and parsnips and the yeast is even happier than ever. This again causes a more constant and reliable fermentation. All these points have been taken care of in the recipes which are designed to produce an abundance of organic matter to give the yeast the best possible conditions short of using the almighty grape.

4

After Fermentation

It will be seen that all recipes end with the direction: 'fit fermentation lock and leave until all fermentation has ceased'. And this is precisely what has to be done. It is a fact that wines never finish fermenting at the same time. Two lots made with the same recipe on the same day containing the same amount of sugar and yeast might finish fermenting weeks apart. Do not let this bother you. People used to baker's yeast might expect wine yeasts to behave in the same fashion, that is, ferment with tremendous vigour and masses of froth and finish fermenting in a few weeks. Wine yeasts do not behave so vulgarly. Being of aristocratic bearing, they behave more sedately. Firstly, they get away to a fairly vigorous fermentation with some frothing and hissing, but not on a par with baker's yeast which is not intended for making wines, but merely for aerating bread.

After a few days of this fairly vigorous ferment, it slows down to what we might call a steady 'ticking over' which might last several months.

As explained in the section dealing with the

fermentation lock, the gas formed passes through the solution in the form of bubbles. After about 10-12 weeks from starting to ferment, it will be found that the solution in the lock has returned to normal – that is, it lies at the bottom of the 'U' bend instead of being pushed up on the out-going side or drawn up in the in-going side.

When this happens it is reasonably safe to say that fermentation has ceased. But do not remove lock and bung down just yet, give it a couple of weeks so that if fermentation starts again – as it often does – there will be no blown bung but merely the fermentation lock working normally again.

Bear in mind that your wine is perfectly safe under the lock and as there is activity of the solution in it all the time, the wisest plan is to leave it alone.

When you are satisfied that fermentation has ceased, remove lock and bung, siphon the clear wine off the deposit into another jar – sterilised, remember – and bung down with a new bung and seal with sealing wax. Put this bunged wine away in a cool place for a year at least if you possibly can. By that time you will have a top-rate wine ready for bottling.

If the wine was not perfectly clear when put into the jar for storing, look at it monthly, and when perfectly clear, siphon it off the deposit into a fresh jar. Bung, seal and store as before.

5

Spoiled Wines

Modern methods – the methods in this book – ensure that wines are not spoiled. Spoilage, as we call it, is caused by using antiquated methods that called for allowing fruits or mixtures of fruit, water and sugar to ferment without added yeast. This method allowed the yeast on the fruit to make the wine. This yeast is known as 'wild' yeast. And while there is usually some good yeast on the fruit with the wild yeast, it was always the wild yeast that seemed to make the wine. Hence the result was very often a beery-tasting wine, low in alcohol; a flat insipid stuff called 'wine' by those who knew no better, or nothing more than a gallon or two of vinegar. If these calamities did not result, the wine was poor in quality, it lacked flavour, had no bouquet at all, was low in alcohol and, by today's standards, was fit only to be poured away. If a fair wine did result, it almost always turned to vinegar on storage.

The reason for all this is easy to understand. Besides there being wild yeasts on the fruits waiting to set up their souring ferments, there is also bacteria in the air waiting to settle on the surface of the wine

37

to turn the small amount of alcohol made into acetic acid – otherwise vinegar.

It is clear from this that we must not only destroy the wild yeasts at the outset, but we must also prevent this yeast and the bacteria just mentioned reaching the fermenting wine and later the bottled product. All this is very simple.

The first inclination of many is to boil the fruits to destroy wild yeast. Boiling will do this, but it nearly always produces a wine which will never clear – no matter how much of how many clarifyers are used. The answer obviously is to use a small amount of harmless chemical that will destroy wild yeasts and allow wines to be made brilliantly clear. This simple means of 'sterilising' the fruit is described in the basic methods for making fruit wines in chapter 9.

Having destroyed the wild yeast on the fruits we now must protect the fermenting wines from wild yeast and bacteria floating about in the air. This is simple enough – but old methods called for allowing the fermenting wine to froth over the sides of the vessel or to be put into loosely corked bottles. This left them open to attacks from both wild yeasts and bacteria, and the result was wines of the sort I have described at the beginning of this section. Now, protecting fermenting wines in the fermenting vessel (polythene pail) is done merely by covering the vessel with a sheet of polythene and tying this down tightly with thin strong string. The gas formed during fermentation often causes this covering to billow up so that you think it will blow itself off. It will not do this because the pressure will force an outlet under the string. This will keep up an outflow of gas so that air and the diseases it carries cannot enter the vessel.

As will be seen in the methods, after the initial vigorous ferment has died down in the fermenting vessel, the still fermenting wine is transferred to jars. At this stage, a fermentation lock is fitted to keep the wine safe during the secondary fermentation which may last as long as three months. The fermentation lock and how to fit it is described and illustrated on page 42.

The wines are, then, protected quite simply. But you would be surprised how many people take these simple precautions to produce the best and then let them go to pot by not sealing the bottled product.

When the wine is finished, matured and brilliantly clear it is bottled. And here, the best safeguard is a flanged (mushroom-shaped) cork and one of the new plastic seals. These are supplied by the gross in tins. And the best way to keep them, if they are supplied in a tin that has to be opened with a tin-opener as they sometimes are, is to pack them into a Kilner jar and screw down tightly. The liquid they are supplied in keeps them expanded. But it will not matter if a few rise above the liquid provided the jar is airtight. When bottling, take one of the seals, slip it over the top of the cork, press down all round and leave it to shrink to make a perfect airtight seal. This it will do in a warm room in a couple of hours.

Now we know how to protect the wine from beginning to end. I have mentioned that wild yeast and bacteria are in the air. Therefore they must be on corks and inside bottles and jars. Ridding our utensils of them is simple. All you need is two two ounces of sodium metabisulphite. Dissolve this in a quart of warm water in a non-metal vessel and then make it up to half a gallon with water. Put this in a half-gallon bottle which almost any chemist will let you have for one shilling. Then, before wine is put into a jar prior to fitting the lock, a pint or so of this solution is poured into the jar; this is shaken so that all the inside is wetted and the solution is poured back into the bulk for further use. The jar should be rinsed afterwards with a little boiled cooled water. This is so that the little solution remaining is washed away. If this were not done, it might harm or even kill the yeast in the still-fermenting wines.

When fermentation is finished and the wine is put into another jar or when it is bottled the same treatment is necessary. But with bottles, a half pint poured into the first and then the next and so on will do. There is no need to use a new half pint for each bottle. When wines that have finished fermenting are put into jars or bottles there is no need to rinse them after using the sterilising solution. Just let them drain upside down for a few minutes.

CORKS

Those little crevices in old corks – and especially those previously used for wine – are teeming with bacteria. Steep them in boiling water for a few minutes. Do this about an hour before bottling time. Then put them in a little of the sterilising solution for a minute or two before using them. It is best to dry them on clean cloth, otherwise they may pop out.

New corks should be put in enough of the solution to cover them for a couple of minutes prior to use.

6

The Fermentation Lock

There are still tens of thousands of people all over the wine-making world who have not yet heard of this, the most valuable piece of equipment ever to reach amateur wine-makers. All it costs is eighteen pence, yet it not only protects wines in jars from attacks from wild yeasts and bacteria, but it also ensures that you get a quality wine.

When this is fitted to a jar of wine as shown in the illustration, the gas formed during fermentation forces its way through the sterilising solution – the same stuff you use to rinse the bottle – in the form of bubbles. The solution closes up automatically so that air and the diseases it carries cannot enter the jar. During the vigorous fermentation stage, bubbles pass through quite rapidly, but after a few weeks, they become fewer and fewer. Later, there may be one an hour and later still only one a day. Later on, when fermentation is nearly finished, the solution stays pushed up on the out-going side for days and nothing seems to be happening. Leave everything as it is. For all the time the solution is pushed up it means that pressure is being generated – if only very

42

slowly. Only when the solution returns to level in the lock should you assume that fermentation has ceased. Even then, it is wise to leave it a week or two longer to see if fermentation should start.

When to fit the lock is given in the methods. It sometimes happens that the solution is seen to be drawn up on the wrong side, that is, it is drawn up on the opposite side to the usual.

This often happens just after the wine has been put into a jar. This is because it may have driven out all air and, because some air must be present between the wine and the bung, some must be drawn in before the lock can work normally. Another cause of this is putting warm wine into a jar or adding warm syrup (sugar-water); the warmth drives out the air so that some must be drawn in. The sterilising solution is there to purify the air drawn back into the jar.

When fermentation has ceased, the solution returns to level in the lock and gradually it is drawn up on the wrong side. After a day or two, it returns to normal.

There are technical – or, I should say, chemical reasons for the fermentation lock being instrumental in the production of quality wines. This has been covered in detail in another work of mine so I cannot cover it here. Let me just assure you that without a fermentation lock you cannot make a quality wine. It improves the alcohol content, the flavour and bouquet.

7

Fermentation Cupboard

A fermentation or fermenting cupboard is not essential, but it makes a great difference to wine-making and wines generally. I made wines for about eighteen years without one and made some top-rate stuff. But for the past nine or ten years I have used a small electrically-heated cupboard fitted with a thermostat and I can honestly say that it has been instrumental in conducting fermentation without a hitch. Gone for me are the days when I imagined wine to be finished, only to find that later the corks blew out and the wine fizzed up all over the place. In many instances, the cork of a jar merely popped out leaving the wine exposed for weeks to all the bacteria and wild yeast that happened to be around. My wines often turned sour or vinegary through this. Another snag was that fermentation would go on endlessly, and while the wines in themselves were good, they could not hope to compete with those I have made since I have used a thermostatically-controlled fermenting cupboard.

They finish fermenting in three months as a rule whatever the outside temperature – whether it be

44

freezing like the devil or not, and they are better wines for this reason. They are fuller-bodied, fermented to the maximum alcohol, whereas they would not be if the temperature varied with the climate. Their flavour is better and they are, for want of better description, better wines altogether.

This idea of a thermostatically-controlled fermenting cupboard might seem expensive. But it is not, and the difference is as great in both work and the finished products, as when you use a lawn mower on your lawn as against a pair of shears.

The cost of the heater and the thermostat is about thirty shillings. This is a black heater – it does not become bright like an electric fire. The 100 watt is ideal. Bear in mind that this is not burning all the time. During winter it might be burning quite a bit, but during spring and summer it is not. It merely warms the cupboard to 65°-70°f. and switches itself off until the temperature drops when it switches itself on again. In so doing, it merely maintains a temperature constant between 65°f. and 70°f.

It is a rough guide to the power consumption to say that it is as cheap as having a 40-watt bulb burning throughout the year. I can honestly say that I have not found any difference in my power bills since I have had one, so it does not cost much to run and anybody can instal it.

An old wardrobe or kitchen cabinet is the ideal for converting to a fermenting cupboard. Either of these would take three shelves each capable of holding three, four or five one-gallon jars. The shelving should be made of strip timber similar to that used in airing cupboards to allow for the warmth to circulate. The heater should go on the floor of the cupboard and the thermostat be hung midway between top and bottom. The first shelf should be about eight inches from the floor – in this way it clears the heater adequately. Subsequent shelving should be spaced to allow room in height for the jars plus fermentation lock.

The converted wardrobe or kitchen cabinet would allow for some forty to fifty gallons of wine to be made a year. A smaller cupboard allowing for three or four one-gallon jars on two shelves (six to eight gallons) fermenting at one time, would allow for twenty-four to thirty-two gallons of wine to be fermented in a year, calculating that four cupboard-fuls could be fermented out in a year – three months for each batch. Even with the smallest number of gallons mentioned here you could make 144 bottles a year or enough for almost three bottles a week, an amount that would normally be plenty for a normal household.

It would not matter where the fermenting cupboard is situated. If you had visited the number of wine-makers I have you would be astonished at the variety of places used for putting the fermenting cupboard. Even bedrooms, bricked-up outside lavatories no longer used and with the main item removed, sheds, outhouses, semi-basements, attics and, in more modern houses and flats, any odd corner big enough. In one flat, I saw the charming polished cupboard arrayed with ornaments and with the television standing on it. This was one enterprising wine-maker's fermenting cupboard.

So you see, it matters not where it goes. And because all jars are fitted with fermentation locks there is no smell of fermenting wine to permeate the house, though perhaps if you have friends in they may wonder what could be causing those mysterious little 'plopping' noises made by the fermentation lock. These would only be heard when everything is quiet, so if you have your fermentation cupboard in the spare bedroom and mother-in-law comes for the week-end, you ought to let her know what to expect otherwise she will think you are trying to frighten her out of the house.

8

Sweet or Dry

As has been seen under 'Fermentation', approximately $2\frac{1}{2}$ lb. sugar are needed in one gallon to produce the usual 14% of alcohol by volume. Therefore, if this amount is used, the wine will be dry provided fermentation has been good and the amount of alcohol that is usually made (14%) is actually produced. This should happen automatically if all goes without a hitch – that is – if the ferment does not stick when a little less than 14% of alcohol has been made. Where more than $2\frac{1}{2}$ lb. of sugar are used the wine will have the usual 14% of alcohol and will be medium dry to medium sweet or sweet according to the amount of sugar used over and above the $2\frac{1}{2}$ lb. used to produce the required alcohol. Where less than $2\frac{1}{2}$ lb. is used per gallon, the wine will not only be dry but also lower in alcohol. And because all dry wines are better for being lower than 14% – usually in the region of 10-12% – it is better when making dry wines to use less than $2\frac{1}{2}$ lb. per gallon. The following table is a useful guide if you propose using more or less sugar than is given in a recipe.

48

Sugar per Gallon		Alcohol by volume	Degrees proof	Type of Wine
lb.	oz.			
1	14	10.5	17.4	Bone dry
2	2	11.9	23	Bone dry
2	10	14.5	24.5	Dry if fermentation good
3	0	15.5	24.5	medium dry to medium sweet according to individual tastes
3	4	14.5	24.5	medium sweet to sweet according to individual tastes
3	8 and above	14.5	24.5	definitely sweet

It will be seen in the recipes that less sugar is used where dried fruit is being used. This is because dried fruits contain approximately 50% sugar: in other words half of each pound of dried fruits amounts to sugar. Therefore, 2 lb. of sugar and a pound of raisins or other dried fruit represents approximately $2\frac{1}{2}$ lb. of sugar – enough for a gallon of dry wine.

Those experimenting of their own accord should bear this in mind otherwise their wines will be sweeter than they want them.

It must also be borne in mind that some wines are better as dry wines than others are. Almost all wines may be sweet, medium or dry according to personal whim, but where you are producing an imitation of a certain commercial product it will have to be either sweet, medium or dry accordingly; and not sweet when it should be dry or vice versa. It is a fact, too, that certain ingredients are more suited to making certain wine types. Some ingredients are especially suitable for making sweet wines while others, while making good dry wines, do not make good sweet wines. I am speaking from the experienced wine-makers point of view now rather than from the beginners. But I do this because many of you will make a gallon or so of certain wine and think to yourselves; well, it's jolly good, but I'm sure it would have been better if it had been dryer, or perhaps in this case it would have been better sweeter. In this event, you have come to your own conclusions just how this particular wine should be made next time. When this stage is reached you will receive my congratulations for you will have reached the stage when you appreciate the fact – an inescapable fact that must come to all wine-makers sooner or later – that, as I have mentioned above, certain ingredients make for certain types of wines and to make the wine sweet when it ought to be dry (or dry when it ought to be sweet) will disappoint.

9

The Use of Clarifiers

My methods of making wines from fresh fruits ensure that top-class, brilliantly clear wines result without the use of clarifiers. But we are not using fresh fruits now and the methods are different. Therefore, we are likely to encounter starch hazes, and sometimes pectin hazes as well, in finished wines. But for heaven's sake do not worry as both can be put right in a moment.

But first, let me explain how the two troubles occur. Fresh fruits contain pectin; it is said that dried fruits do not, but I am sure they do, if only in small amounts. Boiling fresh fruits and pouring boiling water over dried fruits releases the pectin which holds minute solids and yeast in suspension giving the wine what we call pectin cloud.

Roots and some other ingredients contain starch. Boiling brings this starch into the water which will eventually be our wine. As explained in other books of mine, by starving the yeast of sugar in the early stages – that is, giving only half the sugar to the yeast to start with – usually results in the yeast converting the starch to sugar and then fermenting it out, thus leaving a brilliantly clear wine. But we cannot, for a number of reasons too technical to explain here, be sure of this happening. Therefore we may find that we have a starch cloud in wines made from starch-bearing materials.

Years ago, both pectin and starch hazes were an accepted thing: people put up with them thinking that all home-made wines had to be cloudy as a matter of course. The fact that some cleared to brilliance was something of a joyful mystery few people bothered to try to solve.

Today, we do not have to tolerate this cloudiness. For a few pence we can clarify to brilliance very rapidly any wine that is cloudy whether the cloud be caused by starch or pectin.

Pectasin is the name of the clarifier that does the trick. I may be accused of favouritism here, but I cannot help that. I have tried very many clarifiers including the well-known isinglass which will clear one type of cloud and worsen another, and I have found that Pectasin is the best of the lot. It can be added either before fermentation or afterwards. Being a die-hard in the belief that all wines will clear themselves eventually – even though I have to admit that some will not – I like to use this after fermentation has ceased. But you can please yourself.

10

Fortifying or Preserving

I am frequently asked if it is necessary to add spirits to wines in order to preserve them. Many of those asking me have recipes from the past calling for as much as a bottle of brandy per gallon. These recipes, left-overs from Granny's day, referred to brandy costing five shillings a bottle – what a lovely thought!

The answer to whether a wine must be fortified to preserve it is a definite 'no' – provided it has been made well. In this event, there will be sufficient alcohol to preserve.

Unfortunately, not everyone makes as much alcohol as they should in all their wines. Dry wines should not contain too much alcohol. The amount produced by two pounds of sugar per gallon is enough for dry wines because these are traditionally lighter in alcohol than others. Being taken before meals as a rule, they should not be as high in alcohol as others.

Bone-dry wines – that is those made with not more than two and a half pounds of sugar per gallon – will keep well. But even here, keeping dry wines is not necessary because unlike the heavier wines they

53

do not improve over as many years as the heavy sorts. Dry wines are usually used before they are three years old, indeed, they are often used as young as nine months by those who normally keep their wines a long time.

Fortifying is useful where some really top-rate wines are to be put away for over five years. This can prove expensive if done on a large scale. But where just a few bottles or half-bottles are to be put away for long keeping, fortifying does not become prohibitive.

Many operators put a few bottles of selected vintages away each year using about one bottle of Vodka to do this. The result is that they have something really exceptional when a birthday or some other anniversary comes along.

Whisky and brandy are rarely used now because they impart their flavours to the wines, flavours that should not be there. Even in root wines where these spirits were often used, the flavours could not be masked.

Very often I have been offered 'something special' by a friend who I knew could make good wines and no matter how he might have protested if I had told him I could taste the brandy, he would never be able to convince me that he had not added some. The same goes for whisky.

But we have now the ideal medium for fortifying: Vodka. This, having neither colour nor flavour, it may be added to any wine.

There are twenty-six ounces of Vodka to the full bottle costing just over two pounds. The cost is a great deal less if you happen to take your holidays where spirits are cheaper than here. Having experimented a good deal with this I conclude that one to one-and-a-half ounces per half wine bottle is quite sufficient to make all the difference to a good wine intended for keeping over long periods. Two to three ounces are needed to the full-sized wine bottle. Assuming that you would like to put away seventeen half-bottles fortified in this fashion, one bottle of Vodka will do nicely. If this would cost too much, half that number of bottles put away each year would still make a useful store of special wines to some special occasion.

The method of adding this is to prepare bottles in the usual way. Put the measure of spirit in the bottle and fill up with wine. As with all wines, the wine should come to within an inch of where the cork will reach.

Preserving with Campden tablets is, of course, very cheap. This method is used by the trade for the cheaper wines which are not high enough in alcohol to keep well. Adding spirit to these would make them too expensive for it is the spirit content that attracts the tax.

One to two Campden tablets per gallon may be used with a wine of good flavour without fear of this being spoiled. Two tablets is usually enough, and it is better to preserve the gallon or half-gallon rather than the bottle.

When all fermentation has ceased and the wine is clear and siphoned off and the deposit ready for putting away for keeping, take a little of this in a china jug – about half a pint from a gallon or half-gallon. Stand the jug in a saucepan of water and heat the water so that the wine is warmed without it coming into contact with metals. Crush the tablets thoroughly into powder and mix this into the wine, stirring with the bone handle of a knife or some other non-metallic instrument. When the powder is all dissolved the wine may be stirred into the bulk to be treated. To ensure thorough mixing, it would be better to put the treated wine into an empty gallon jar and fill up with the rest of the wine.

And don't forget, one tablet should be enough for half a gallon – two for one gallon.

II

Wines for Slimmers

There are a number of reasons for certain people not being allowed to drink sweet wines or even the less sweet wines simply because they contain sugar. It may be that they are slimming or for medical reasons are not permitted to take sugar. Provided they are not prevented for any reason from taking alcohol, they may take all the sweet wines they like when sweetened as I recommend here.

Those who like the bone-dry wines need not sweeten them, but those who like a sweet wine, but must not take sugar, should make all their wines bone dry by using not more than 2 lb. of sugar per gallon. This will be fermented out, leaving a bone-dry wine – wine containing no sugar. They may then sweeten the wine to taste with saccharin. The best way is to let the wine become a completely finished product bottled for storing and then, when a bottle is required for use, the cork may be removed and the tablet dropped in. When this is dissolved, the wine may be tasted. It may need a half-tablet more, or a whole one, depending on personal tastes.

The saccharin cannot ferment so there is no risk of a secondary fermentation, but do keep the wines corked and sealed while in store and well corked when opened and in use.

It will be seen that I have recommended not more than 2 lb. of sugar per gallon for wines to be treated with saccharin by those who must not take sugar. As will be seen in the sugar table, this amount of sugar makes approximately 11·9% of alcohol – almost 12% – and by using this amount we can be absolutely certain that all of it is fermented out. But this amount of alcohol is not enough to preserve the wine, so careful storage is essential. Treating the wine with Campden solution (Campden tablets) to preserve it is not recommended in this case as there might be some undesirable reaction of the Campden solution on the saccharin, or the saccharin on the Campden solution. But if you make these wines for those who must not take sugar and sweeten them with saccharin, and then keep them stored properly and well-corked while in use, there is no reason at all why everything should not go according to plan.

IMPORTANT NOTE

It should be born in mind that dried fruit contain sugar. 1 lb. raisins and most other dried fruit contain 50% sugar. Therefore, if a recipe calls for $2\frac{1}{2}$ lb. sugar and 1 lb. raisins the overall amount of sugar that will go into the must is 3 lb. Therefore, because only two pounds per gallon must be used, the sugar in the recipe must be reduced to $1\frac{1}{2}$ lb. The half pound in the raisins or other dried fruit will make up the other half pound. A little quick and careful calculating in this direction will soon put you right when using various recipes. Where necessary, a special note about this aspect will be included.

12

After-Care and Storing

It is a lamentable fact that having gone to some trouble to make top-class wines many people let them spoil.

Perhaps this is a fault of those who write on the subject; we seem so keen to show how good wines are to be made that we forget to tell you how to keep them. So let me give a little guidance. All my recipes and directions end with 'and leave until all fermentation has ceased'. And it is reasonable to suppose that most people would ask – what do I do now?

When fermentation has ceased the wine should be siphoned of the deposit into a freshly sterilised jar, bunged down tightly with a new bung and put away in a cool place for at least a year.

If the wine was brilliantly clear when put into the storage jar, there will be no need to look at it. But if it was not quite clear, it would be wise to test for clarity. If in a glass jar, all one need do is to wipe the jar free of dust with a damp cloth and hold it to light or shine a fairly powerful torch through it. If brilliantly clear and with only a very slight

59

deposit the wine may be left until it has been in store for one year. If the deposit is, say, a quarter inch thick, it would be best to siphon the clear wine into bottles, as to leave a heavy deposit might give the wine 'off' flavours. If you have several gallons of a particular wine and not just one gallon, the clear wine should be transferred to other jars, but a little will be left in each jar so that the last one-gallon jar will have to be used to for filling up. This will mean that there might be only a half gallon left in the last jar to be emptied. You may either put this in a half-gallon jar or bottle it for immediate use. Bear in mind that it is always safest to fill jars to within about an inch and a half of where the bung will reach. Therefore, where less than a gallon remains after racking – this means taking wine off deposit – it would be better to put half in a half-gallon jar and the rest in bottles.

Where stone jars are in use, you cannot see whether the wine is clear or not or how much deposit there might be. This problem can be overcome quite simply by inserting a length of glass tubing of about a quarter-inch bore or less. Put it in, holding it upright, until it reaches bottom. Then press the thumb over the open end, and, holding tightly with the thumb pressed firmly in place, carefully withdraw the tube. The tube will contain a sample of your wine from top to bottom of the jar – including the deposit. From this sample you will be able to see whether the wine is clear all the way down or not and the thickness of the deposit, and be able to decide whether to rack it or leave it a bit longer. When brilliantly clear wine is put away for keeping there will be no need to rack for at least two years unless you want to use the wine. Clear wines do sometimes throw a deposit, but this sort of deposit does no harm. It is the deposit from unclear wines which gives 'off' flavours. Therefore, if brilliant wine is put into stone jars there will be no need to look at it from time to time.

Knowing how to look after wines in this way is important for it prevents good wines being spoiled on storing.

But storing is equally important and not as easy in a modern house or flat as in older houses, though it need not be the chore some people make it. Writing on this aspect in a magazine I said that every house has a cupboard under the stairs. This promptly brought a letter from someone who hadn't, but provided you do have one, your storing problem should resolve itself. If this has a stone floor as many do, so much the better. If not, two or three paving stones laid discreetly and the jars of wine stood on these will keep down the temperature of the cupboard and also keep the wine cool.

If there is no cupboard under the stairs you will have to look elsewhere. Where just small amounts are made and these used up fairly quickly, almost anywhere will do provided the wine does not become over-warm. Bear in mind that the north side of the house is always coolest and that an area low down is always cooler than one high up. Therefore use the floor whenever you can in preference to shelving, even if it is merely the floor of the built-in wardrobe in the spare bedroom.

The real do-it-yourself enthusiast, making some hundred gallons a year as many do, will have his storing problems. But these chaps, and I know plenty of them, use their imagination and turn out wine stores in the most unlikely places. Living not far from me is an ardent wine-maker with a cellar in the attic. He has insulated this against heat; this, of course, insulates it against cold. And in this he has row upon row of two, three and four-gallon jars of some really worthwhile wines. With floor and lighting, it is no trouble to bottle some of his wine and to bring down a few bottles at a time. If you are thinking of putting up a shed or garage or even a greenhouse, it would be worth considering putting in a false floor. A pit a few feet long and wide and about two feet deep could be taken out and lined with bricks or concrete The wine is then put in and a trapdoor cut in the shed floor to enable you to reach the wine. If this were done in a real workman-like fashion the resulting 'cellar' would be ideal.

Coolness is an important factor of successful storage, but this is not of overriding importance where the temperature is fairly constant. What is most important is that it does not vary too much. Freezing one day and very hot the next would cause calamity, but where the temperature does not vary greatly, wines may be stored quite safely.

Dark-coloured and especially red wines should be stored in the dark or kept in stone jars and then put into dark-coloured bottles. This is because light penetrating red wines often spoils them. The lighter-coloured wines may be put into clear glass bottles and these will come to no harm if light reaches them.

I am sure the main consideration when storing wines is non-disturbance. I say this because when a wine is a finished product, brilliantly clear, free of all deposit, bunged and sealed, it should be put away and left *undisturbed* for the time needed for it to mature.

This will vary with the type of wine and the variety and amount of ingredients used. Light wines, dry wines and those of lower alcohol content will not need more than a year, but the heavier types will need two or three years. Three to five years is normally the longest home-made wines will keep safely. I say 'normally' because under our very ordinary circumstances we cannot hope to give them similar conditions as the trade can give theirs; further, we are not using the almighty grape which is supposed to make 'true' wines only, all others being substitutes.

When I say keep safely, I really mean continue to improve and not disappoint upon opening. I do not mean that over five years old they will go 'off'.

It is a fact that many home-made wines will continue to improve for up to ten years and then keep to the pinnacle of perfection for a further ten years. But it is equally true that some will improve for up to five years and then begin to lose their quality. Therefore, it would be wise not to keep your wines for more than five years, but you could put a bottle or two away for ten years if you want to just to prove me wrong.

If you do this, or if you open wines stored for three or four years or longer, and find them 'flat' and lifeless, do not consign them to the drain and curse poor me. For the chances are that all these wines need is decanting.

DECANTING

This serves a dual purpose. Wines stored over long periods in dark, airless conditions do become life-less, and, upon opening, are really disappointing. But this is merely the result of having stored them under bad conditions, as opposed to their having lost their quality through over-ageing.

Decanting gives you the opportunity to see what has happened – whether the wine has lost its quality – or has merely lost it temporarily owing to storage. It also gives you the chance to put bottled wines into other bottles or a decanter free of any deposit that may have formed. There can be nothing more em-barrassing than to pour wines for friends and to find that half-way through the bottle, the wine comes over cloudy.

Wines intended for use, say, within a day or so should be bottled if in jars, or re-bottled if already in bottles. The airing puts life into wines that have lost it through storing so that what appears to be a flat and lifeless wine takes on that robust freshness, and all-round good flavour and bouquet we expect from wines of quality.

Even wines on the point of losing their quality through over-ageing will be improved temporarily by decanting. Such wines should be used up fairly quickly – say within a couple of months.

13

Blending

Many years ago I regarded blending wines as cheating – not others, but myself. I felt that if I could not make good wines without having to blend them to get what I wanted, I ought not to be making them at all. I should, I argued, be able to make good wines from whatever ingredients I might be using. It did not occur to me at that time that blending is the only means of obtaining special results.

Some people blend ingredients before they make the wine; thus we have several ingredients rather than merely one. The one has now become the main ingredient with others blended in to get some special result.

For example, many years ago one merely used potatoes with a couple of lemons to give the necessary acid into the must. Someone blended the result with a raisin wine. They liked it and decided to add raisins next time they made potato wine. Later, they blended the result with orange wine and, again, liked it. So they added a couple of oranges to the recipe. Thus, to the main ingredients – potatoes and lemons – was added both raisins and oranges to

65

make something really special and a new recipe had been evolved.

But the resulting wine, while being very good, would have been better if three separate wines had been made and blended later. In this case, the three would have been the original potato wine, the raisin wine and the orange wine. The reason I say it would have been better is because the blending could have been controlled to give a finer flavour. But having lumped all ingredients together, one had to accept the result, because to blend any other wine with a wine already made with so many ingredients would have given rise to a confusion of flavours, so that hardly anybody would be able to decide the type of flavour they could taste or the sort of wine they were tasting.

Had three separate wines been made and then blended carefully, the flavour of raisin or orange would have been allowed to predominate, while the ordinary potato wine – or some of it – could have been left as it was.

Further, when blending these, some of the raisin and the orange wines could have been kept back for use as they were.

Blending is an art easily acquired and there is no reason for anyone shirking it. It is not only a means of making something really special, but is also a means of ironing out faults and improving disappointments.

Let me deal with the faults first. Many of you will make wines with recipes other than those here and it could be that some turn out too acid while others turn out not acid enough or lack flavour. Carefully balanced recipes will not make wines with these faults, but, unfortunately, there are countless recipes in circulation that do.

Over-acid wines may be blended with those lacking acid and vice-versa provided they are similar wines. By this I mean that there must be some similarity in the two (or three) wines being blended. It would be disastrous, for example, to blend rhubarb wine with any wines made with red fruits or dried fruits with the exception perhaps of sultana wine. But rhubarb wine often blends well with certain root wines.

Dried fruit wines blend well together – raisin with prune and so on. In fact, all dried-fruit wines blend well with each other, peach will go well with apricot, sultana wine blends with either apricot or peach wine, but not with a blend of these wines.

Over-sweet wines may be blended with dry wines of similar type. Similarly, wines that have turned out too dry may be blended with over-sweet wines to strike a balance.

Wine made with synthetic must only, blends with almost any wine and is useful for reducing flavours where these have become too pronounced when too much of a certain ingredient has been used unwittingly. It is also useful for reducing over-sweetness or over acidity, but do go carefully in these cases, because, having little flavour of its own, it will reduce the strength of flavour of any wine it is added to. It is useful to have a gallon or a few bottles of this wine in store for the purpose of rectifying faults of this sort. Bear in mind that the flavours given into wines by T'Noirot extract will *not* blend with each other. Therefore, do not blend wines made with these. But if a fault needs rectifying – which

I shall very much doubt – it may be put right by blending with wine made with synthetic must only.

Do not attempt blending when time is short. Decide in advance the wines you want to try this with and set them aside. Then, when you have plenty of time, set about this simple task with interest.

The best plan is to start with blending two wines. Later you can blend three or four if you want to but do not blend for the sake of it. This will merely result in producing something quite the reverse of what you expected.

Having decided which wines you think would go well together, put a measured amount of the main wine or basic wines into a glass and add a measured amount of the wine to go with it. Sample this, and if this is what you want, you will know from the measures how much of each to put together.

It is wise to use a fluid ounce measure for this job. Put a fluid ounce of the basic wine into a glass and half an ounce of the second wine into this; stir with a cocktail stick and sample. This measure will mean that the blending is two to one, two half fluid ounces of the basic wine to one fluid ounce of the second. Therefore, if you are going to do it on a large scale the answer here is two bottles of the basic wine with one of the second wine. If a second sampling is required take a little cheese and chew well and, having swallowed this, sample after each addition. This is necessary in order to clean the palate so that small differences in flavour are noticeable whereas they might not be if the palate contained the taste of the previous sample.

Do not blend indiscriminately and without due

thought. I say this because many wines thought to be not up to expectations are usually first-class wines of their type. It is all a matter of what you intend to use them for. If you are the kind of person who uses wines only in the evening, the heavier and more mellowed wines will be more to your liking. The sharper – those slightly acid wines – and the astringent sorts will not necessarily be to your liking. These taken before meals can do wonders both to the meal and to the appetite. The practice of taking wines with meals is growing over here owing to so many people taking continental holidays. Therefore, the aim when making wines and when blending should be to produce wines of many sorts, suitable for all occasions and not just one or two for evening use.

When blending, rinse the glass free of each sample and dry before putting another sample into it, or use several glasses. If the glass contains dregs of the previous sample the next sample will be thrown out of balance.

Do this simple job with a workmanlike approach and there is nothing to prevent you making some really unique and very excellent blends.

14

Wines from Concentrated Grape Juice

A wide variety of top-class wines may be made from the grape concentrates now available to everybody. At first glance these wines may appear expensive, but they are not, because they are the very finest wines provided they are made well. Top-class wines always cost more than others, but even these are not expensive when one considers that they are made from the true wine-making materials.

Using grape concentrate is just the same as using grapes fresh from the vine except that you have pure grape juice with all water extracted, so that you have sufficient grape juice in one quart of concentrate to make one gallon of wine – or about the amount of juice produced by twelve to fourteen pounds of grapes.

All that need be done to return the concentrate to its natural state – that is pure grape juice free of pips and skins – is to add the same amount of water that was taken from it in order to concentrate it.

Thus a quart of juice is made into one gallon by adding water and you have the true material for making wines from grapes.

There are many concentrates available. Some from southern France, some from Spain, some from Cyprus and so on. All make wines of differing types. For example the Cyprus grape is different from those of Spain; thus the wines will be different. There are white concentrates and red and intermediate. All make absolutely top-rate wines.

Unfortunately, I cannot say which I have found the best, for each makes a different wine type and it is for you to decide which type of wine you want to make.

It is merely a matter of deciding whether to make the wines famous in Spain or Cyprus or whether to make the heavier red or white port styles by using the dark red or white concentrates. Firms dealing in these (see Appendix) will be glad to advise you.

Several different wines may be made from one gallon of concentrate; for example you can make four separate gallons – one sweet, one medium, one light and dry and another heavier and dry. On the other hand, you can make the one gallon of concentrate into one type of wine if you want to.

A trial quart, costing about 12/6, will make one gallon of top-class wine of the type made from the grapes from the area in which they were grown.

This type of wine-making is gaining enormous popularity not only because of the type and the quality of the wine but because, being ready to use, there is no preparation of ingredients to bother about. In addition is the fact that the finished product, costing about 2/6 per bottle to produce, is worth 12/6 to 15/- per bottle. Even if you decide to fortify some of these with Vodka (See Preserving and Fortifying, p. 53) the addition of 2/- worth of the spirit would not make them too expensive in relation to their type and quality. Where for example could you buy a top-rate full-bodied wine of excellent flavour and bouquet at 4/6 a bottle?

I must hasten to add that fortifying is NOT necessary, but many people like to do this with just a few bottles once or twice a year.

Let me suppose you have one quart of one of concentrated grape juices and want to make this into one gallon of wine. This will be simpler than showing how to make one gallon of juice into four different gallons of various wines – I will touch upon this part later.

To make this quart into one gallon of must, all you need do is to boil three quarts of water and allow it to cool, then stir in the concentrate, add yeast and nutrient and let it ferment in the fermenting vessel for five-six days in the same way as for other wines.

After this, it is put into a gallon jar, a fermentation lock is fitted and the wine allowed to ferment to completion. After which it is treated as any other wine.

The resulting wine will be bone dry and of about 12% of alcohol by volume (approx. 19.5° proof). This is plenty for a dry wine: indeed, most commercially-produced dry wines are in the region of 9-11% by volume. A greater percentage of alcohol in a dry wine would render it almost unpalatable to everybody except those few who regard a high percentage of alcohol as the most important thing, which it is not.

So, if you want a dry wine, there is nothing more to do. But if you want a higher percentage of alcohol and a less dry to sweeter wine, some sugar will have to be added, and this must be done sometime during the process.

Therefore, if you want to add sugar for the reasons just stated, you must not use three quarts of water at the start, but save one pint of it.

Then, when the wine is put into a jar after the few days fermentation in the covered vessel, the sugar may be boiled for a few minutes in the pint of water and when cooled added to the wine as syrup.

As we have seen, the grape juice contains enough sugar to produce 12% of alcohol by volume and because all this will be fermented out in the making of that 12% we must add enough to make 14% – the amount the yeast will make – and still a little more so that this is left unfermented to sweeten the wine.

For a medium wine add 12 oz. sugar to that kept-back pint and boil it for two minutes and add, as already advised, when cool. To make a sweeter wine add 1 lb. of sugar as above.

If these amounts of sugar are added according to the sort of wine you want, the wines will contain 14% of alcohol by volume (approx. 26° proof), and will be either medium or sweet depending on the amount of sugar added.

It will be seen from the above that to make one gallon of wine from that quart of concentrate is a very simple matter indeed.

It is equally simple to make four separate gallons of differing wines from one gallon of concentrate, or two sorts of wine from a half gallon.

All you need do with the one gallon is to divide it into four quarts. To one quart add three quarts of boiled cooled water, add yeast and nutrient, and ferment it out as a dry wine. To the second quart you could add 12 oz. sugar, as advised earlier, to make a medium and to the third quart add 1 lb. of sugar, as advised, to make a sweet wine. With the fourth quart you might like to try one of the recipes on pages 126-9. Where I show how to make your concentrate go further by using a little dried fruit.

From all this will be seen that if you invest in a half gallon of concentrate you can make two separate gallons of dry, or medium, or medium and sweet or merely dry and sweet.

The amounts of sugar given above are in consideration of the fact that most concentrated grape juices contain enough sugar to produce 12% of alcohol by volume when a quart is made into a gallon. Bear in mind that the same results when a half gallon is made into two gallons or when one gallon is made into four gallons.

Unfortunately, all concentrates do not contain the same amounts of sugar. And it will be seen from various advertisements issued by home wine-making supply firms that their concentrate has a specific gravity of 1·385, or whatever it might be. But whether it has, in fact, this specific gravity, is another matter. And since the figure quoted is the key to the amount of sugar the concentrate contains, it is important to be sure.

The surest means of finding out the sugar content of the concentrate is to use a hydrometer. This is a simple instrument to use where exact results are essential. Those prepared to take a chance on whether their wines turn out a little drier or less sweet than they expected will not want to bother with it.

But those who want to know in advance precisely the amount of alcohol they will make and the exact amount of sugar they want to leave unfermented to sweeten the wine will have to use one.

USING THE HYDROMETER

Specific gravity. This merely means, as compared with water. Water has the gravity of 1·000. Since we are concerned with the amount of sugar in a concentrate we see at once that the grape juice has a much higher gravity and in the figure quoted (1·385) we see that as compared with water the grape juice is ·385 degrees higher. This figure represents the amount of sugar contained in the concentrate, and the figure will be the same whether you buy a quart or a gallon.

As I have mentioned, some concentrates may be a little higher in reading while others may be a little lower. But whatever the figure, only the figure above the 1·000 represents the sugar content.

Now take that figure ·385: we call this when set out alone – that is without the 1· in front which represents water which we are using as a comparison – the gravity. Therefore a concentrate having a specific gravity of 1·385 has the gravity of ·385 – often written as 385.

Now let us suppose we have a quart (or a gallon) of concentrate which the retailers says has the gravity of 385 (specific gravity 1·385). If we make this into one gallon with boiled cooled water we should get a reading on the hydrometer of a quarter of that figure because we have made four times as much of the concentrate. But we shall not get a quarter of the figure 1·385 because the water we add already has the gravity of 1·000. But we shall get a reading of a quarter of the figure above the 1·000, in this case ·385. This is because this figure represents the sugar content of the concentrate and we shall have reduced this by four by making four times as much of the concentrate. Therefore a quart (or gallon) with a gravity of ·385 will have the gravity 096 when made into four times as much with water. And this figure of 096 will be representing the sugar content of the juice diluted ready for making into wine. As compared with water the juice now has the specific gravity of 1·096. To make it absolutely clear look at it this way:

water	1·000
sugar	96
specific gravity	1·096

If you will now take a look at the Hydrometer table on page 76, you will see that this figure of 096 represents sufficient sugar to make just over 12% of alcohol by volume – though the actual figure 096 is not given.

HYDROMETER TABLE

Specific gravity	Gravity	Potential Alcohol by volume per cent	Degrees proof
1·080	080	10·5	17·4
1·090	090	11·9	19·5
1·100	100	13·4	22·9
1·110	110	14·5	24·5

Most people will want to add sugar to get the higher readings so that they get a higher alcohol content. And if we bear in mind that the yeast will make under favourable conditions the maximum – 14·5% by volume – we shall see that we have to raise the gravity from 096 to 110 to get the maximum reading.

If you would be content with less alcohol you need as less sugar.

Bear in mind that $2\frac{1}{4}$ oz. of sugar represents $5°$ on the hydrometer. Therefore to raise the reading from 1·096 to 1·110 (raise it $14°$ – let's call it $15°$) we need to add three times $2\frac{1}{4}$ oz. $= 6\frac{3}{4}$ oz. per gallon.

As has been seen, this reading represents the amount of sugar needed to make 14·5 of alcohol by volume, and as this will be used up leaving a dry wine it will be necessary to add a few ounces more to leave some unfermented to sweeten. In the normal way, four to six ounces of sugar per gallon is all that is needed to sweeten. This may be added when you have added the amount needed to raise the reading or at some later stage.

If you could rely on the claim that the grape juice has a certain specific gravity you could work all this out without having to use the hydrometer at all as we have just done.

But it is a fact that the specific gravity is often wide of the stated figure. And if you work it all out assuming the figure to be correct the result would be anything but what you hoped for.

Therefore, if you want to be exact you should use a hydrometer to make sure the concentrate has the figure stated and if not adjust it by adding sugar to suit your requirements.

Hydrometers with trial jars are obtainable from all home wine supply firms (see Appendix) quite inexpensively. The trial jar can be dispensed with if you have a very tall lager glass.

To avoid having to use two hydrometers it is best to work in the following manner, but first obtain a hydrometer reading from 1·100 to 1·200.

You have your concentrate ready and want to be sure how much sugar it contains – or will contain when it has been made into four times as much with added water. You cannot test the concentrate itself because your hydrometer does not cover a high enough range of figures.

So, make the concentrate into twice as much by adding a quart of boiled cooled water to each quart of concentrate. Mix the grape juice and water well. Put the hydrometer into the trial jar or lager glass and pour in the mixture until the hydrometer floats free of all parts of the jar. Make sure the jar is on a level surface. Note where the juice cuts across the stem of the hydrometer. The figure shown will be the specific gravity of the diluted concentrate. Let us say that this figure is 1·192. It could be more and it could be less – but this will do for the moment. From this it will be seen that when this half gallon is made into one gallon the figure above the 1·000 which represents the sugar content will be reduced by half again. So without further testing you will know that the figure ·192 will be reduced to ·096. This will mean that when diluted to its full extent the specific gravity of the grape juice ready for making into wine will be 1·096.

As I have said, the figure could be more or it could be less depending on the sugar content of the concentrate. If it were 1·160 at the testing stage you would know that it will be 1·080 when diluted fully.

The advantage of knowing what the sugar content is before the juice is diluted fully enables you to work out how much sugar to add to get the alcohol content you want before the concentrate is diluted to the full. For example if you have already made a quart of grape juice into a gallon and want to add sugar you would have to boil this in extra water and so dilute the concentrate more than is desirable.

But by knowing in advance you are able to work out how much sugar to add by working in the following manner.

Let us suppose at test the concentrate is one of the figures quoted, say 1·192. You know that when this is made into twice as much the figure will be 1·096. From the table you will see that this sugar content will make approximately 12% of alcohol by volume. If this is enough, all you need do is to make it twice as much with boiled cooled water, add yeast and nutrient and ferment it right out to a dry wine.

But if you want more alcohol you must save a pint of the water for boiling the amount of sugar you want to add.

So you add three pints of water to make the now half gallon up to nearly a gallon and add yeast and nutrient and get fermentation under way. Then after say five or six days fermentation, you work out how much sugar you want to add, boil it in the kept-back pint of water and when cool add it to the rest. Thereafter the wine is treated in the normal way.

As I have mentioned 2¼ oz. of sugar will raise the reading in one gallon by 5°.

Therefore, if you know that you must increase the reading from 1·080 to 1·110 to get the alcohol you want, you must increase it by 30°: that is add 2¼ oz. sugar to each five degrees, but in this case six – six fives being thirty. Therefore the sugar to add is six times two-and-a-quarter ounces – 13½ oz. After this, you will have to add a little more sugar so that some is left unfermented to sweeten the wine and this, of course, may be boiled with the necessary addition.

The same applies to all measures whether you are making a quart of concentrate into a gallon of wine or whether you are making a gallon into four gallons. The 2¼ oz. sugar to 5° ratio relates to one gallon. If two gallons are being sugared you would need 4½ oz. to raise the gravity by 5°. If four gallons are being sugared you would need nine ounces to raise the reading by 5°.

All this is very simple when you have the hydrometer at hand and have made the concentrate into twice as much with boiled cooled water and mixed well. I will repeat the simple formula for the sake of simplicity.

Having made the concentrate into twice as much, you take the reading as already mentioned. From this reading you will know that when you have made this into twice as much again, the figure above the 1·000 will be halved. And this figure is the specific gravity of the mixture when it is diluted to its full extent. Therefore, you work out how many five degrees there are between this reading and the reading relating to the amount of alcohol you want to make (see alcohol table, p. 76). You then boil 2¼ oz.

to each 5° on the hydrometer in some of the total water to be used and when cool add to the rest.

On page 151 is an illustration of the hydrometer floating in a sample must and showing a specific gravity of 1·045.

It will be clear from this that if the must contained more sugar, the hydrometer would not be able to sink so low because the must would be thicker and a higher reading would be registered.

This hydrometer does not cover the range of the one you will be using. Yours, reading from 1·100 to 1·200, is for use before the must is diluted to its full extent. The one in the illustration is the sort normally used for must diluted to their full extent.

As explained earlier, I have worked it out for you while using the higher reading hydrometer to avoid using two hydrometers and also so that you know before you have diluted to the full extent, the amount of sugar you need to add.

Testing for Alcohol Content

When using the hydrometer you are able to find whether you have made the amount of alcohol you want. For example, if you want 14·5% you will add the necessary sugar to give you a reading of 1·110 when the must is diluted to the full. As this is the amount of alcohol normally made you should, when all fermentation has ceased, have a hydrometer reading of 1·000. This is because all the sugar has been fermented out. It is just possible that you would get a reading of just below a thousand because the presence of alcohol makes the wine 'thinner' than water – and it is water we are using as a comparison, remember.

But let us say that the final reading should be 1·000. If it is higher than this when you began with a reading of 1·110, it means that you have not made quite all the alcohol you should. If it is only a couple of degrees above 1·000 it will not matter, but if it is 10 to 15, you should leave the wine in a warm place in order to get fermentation on the go again if you want to. But if satisfied with the result, there is no need to do this. When you have added sugar to give you a reading of 1·110 and then some more for sweetening purposes, bear in mind that the amount used for sweetening will not be fermented out and will register on the hydrometer when all fermentation has ceased.

For example. If you began with a reading of 1·110 and then added say, 4½ oz. of sugar to sweeten the wine, that 4½ represents 10° on the hydrometer. So, in effect, you started with a specific gravity 1·120. But because the yeast can use only the amount of sugar represented by the figure ·110, the sweetening sugar (10° in this case) remains. But this does not matter because the ·110 representing the amount of sugar needed to make the alcohol you want will have been used and you will have a reading on completion of fermentation of 1·010. This 10° represents the amount of sugar used for sweetening.

15

The Use of T'Noirot Extracts

In an earlier work of mine I described – indeed, introduced for the first time ever – the use of T'Noirot extracts. Just what these are will be described later on. Just let me say here that these are now becoming very popular for with them we make wines flavoured of all the world-famous liqueurs, Vermouth, both French and Italian style, and also syrups and genuine liqueurs as well if we want to. In the earlier work, the details were for using extracts alone with water, yeast and sugar. This combination gave me first-class results. Unfortunately, fermentation took a very long time owing to lack of organic matter, details of which appear under the heading 'Yeast'.

Many people were content to wait fifteen months and even longer for fermentation to cease, but others were not so patient. I therefore set out to evolve recipes using ingredients that would produce very little flavour of their own in order that they would not interfere with the flavours given into the wines by the extract, yet at the same time produce organic matter essential to a quality wine and a short fermentation period of three months or so. For the benefit of those thinking of experimenting on their own accord, let me say that to use strongly flavoured fruits such as elderberries or blackberries would be a waste of time and money because (although these produce an abundance of organic matter), even if little fruit were used, you would have difficulty in masking their flavour. Using more extract would not be the answer. This would merely make the wines too expensive and quite unpalatable in any case, owing to the great strength of flavour you would have to obtain in order to mask the flavour of the fruits.

In some recipes it will be seen that we *are* able to use fresh fruits with certain extracts – notably a few peaches and apricots with a peach and apricot extract. Now these fruit are usually expensive or scarce or both for most people, but by using small quantities of fresh fruits to give organic matter as well as flavour, together with a small amount of extract, they are able to make their favourite wines more easily and more cheaply than when fresh fruit alone is used. In other cases, notably Vermouth and a few others, it was essential not to use ingredients with flavours difficult to mask, because no ingredient I know of would go alongside the Vermouth flavour as true in using peaches and peach extract.

Another reason for evolving recipes was that many people do not like using invert sugar; heaven knows why! When carrying out my early trials with these extracts using water sugar and yeast only, invert sugar gave me much better results than household sugar. Yet household sugar gives absolutely excellent results when there is a small amount of organic matter present as in the recipes in this book. The amounts of sugar given in the recipes are for household sugar. Those using invert sugar – as many experienced wine-makers do – bear in mind that this contains moisture and that one and a quarter pounds must be used for every one pound of household sugar given in the recipes. It is perhaps a bit elementary to warn that you should choose as your first attempt an extract whose flavour you are familiar with, yet you would be surprised how many people would overlook this. Not everybody likes Vermouth and hardly anybody could hope to be familiar with all the flavours available. So choose carefully and avoid disappointment.

T'Noirot Extracts – What They Are

Firstly I must stress that these are not synthetic, nor are they essences. They are the genuine flavours of the liqueurs the name of which they carry – in so far as they can be. I add this because the flavours of many liqueurs are closely guarded secrets. We all have heard of the world-famous secret of the Benedictine Monks – Benedictine. It is said that this flavour is obtained by about five herbs and that a dozen or more others are thrown in to create nothing more than confusion amongst those who want to find the basic secret. And so it goes with many others. Yet these extracts do give the flavours they claim to and are either of herb or fruit base and are therefore neither essences nor synthetic.

It will be seen that in many cases there are more than one recipe and method for making a particular wine using an extract. This is because while one recipe or method or basic ingredient will appeal to one reader another will prefer to use a different one.

For example some will go headlong for using potatoes or parsnips as the basic ingredient while others will not want to bother with them: these will go for the raisins or sultanas or dates. It is merely a matter of choice: my experience leaves me with only one doubt – which basic ingredient produces the best results. Frankly, I cannot say with the absolute certainty I would like to be able to. This is probably owing to the fact that the basic ingredient, or the amount used, which is quite small by ordinary wine-making standards, is not sufficient to make a good quality wine in its own right. In other words, if only the basic materials were used, the wine would lack flavour, bouquet and fullness. The basic ingredient I must stress if only for the purpose emphasis is used as a base – as organic matter to assist yeast reproduction and therefore help to make the maximum alcohol in the shortest possible time.

Most people will already be familiar with at least three or four of the flavours of the extracts through having used liqueurs or Vermouth at sometime or other, and will know at once which flavour they are going to use. Any reader not quite sure of himself in this respect should get a sample of say six bottles and make a basic wine – any of those with a potato or parsnip base will do – and when this is a finished product, bottled and clear, a little extract may be put into each bottle. In this way, he will make six different flavoured wines from the one base and be able to decide which flavours he likes most and then make the wine in bulk. If you do this, go very carefully with the extract as very little is needed to flavour a bottle of wine. And do not expect such good results as when the extract is fermented with the rest of the ingredients. When talking to various wine-making clubs and circles and other interested bodies, I take along samples of the wines I have made with the recipes in this book and everywhere they are acclaimed as first rate.

NOTE

In the recipes the amounts of extract to use is given in fluid ounces. The beginner might be put off by this, so let me explain about the bottle sizes. The small bottles contain half a fluid ounce while the larger (used by many people to flavour one gallon) contain one-and-two-thirds fluid ounces. Either way, two fluid ounces is usually enough to flavour one gallon where no flavour is obtained from the basic material, for example, where potatoes or raisins or other roots or dried fruits are used. But where the basic material is a fruit of similar flavour to the extract – peaches with a peach extract for example – less than one fluid ounce is usually enough.

For this reason it would be well worthwhile getting a fluid ounce measure from a chemist. The small plastic ones give teaspoons, tablespoons and fluid ounces and cost about 1/6. You will find that two tablespoons make one fluid ounce. Therefore if you happen to have a tablespoon measure, this will do. On no account use a tablespoon from a cutlery drawer as these are not necessarily anything like the correct measure. I understand that Woolworths and other multiple stores retail suitable measures very cheaply. All this may seem to complicate matters, but I assure you that this is not so – nothing could be simpler than making wines with the recipes here.

16

Wines — Not Liqueurs

It is important to understand at the outset that wines made from the recipes in this chapter are wines in the strictest sense and NOT liqueurs. The fact that they bear the name of the liqueur they resemble might mislead one or two readers to imagine that they are as strong as liqueurs. But a quick glance at other pages will show that all wines made from recipes in this book will be in the region of 14% by volume, or less where little sugar is used as has already been explained. Because true liqueurs range from 40° proof to as high as 75° proof and sometimes even higher, home-made wines cannot hope to compete with them in alcohol content.

Therefore, the wines made from recipes here will be of good alcohol content for wines generally, regardless of the fact that they are flavoured by the liqueurs whose name they will still carry. This is not the place for lengthy discourse on liqueurs. These are dealt with in the appropriate chapter.

Recipes for Using T'Noirot Extracts

The amounts of sugar given in the recipes that follow are those I use myself for the various wines. Those who know from experience that they must have their wines bone dry – regardless of type of wine being made – should consult the short table on page 49.

Potatoes and parsnips should be old. End of season potatoes used in May and June are best and if these have long sprouts on them so much the better, discard the sprouts before using the potatoes. Parsnips *may* be used quite fresh, but I have found that wines made from parsnips that have been out of the soil for some time clear more readily. Stored home-grown parsnips used in March and later are even better. Use King Edward potatoes if you possibly can, as these, I have found, not only make for a better wine in itself, but the wine clears very quickly after fermentation has ceased.

As all the ingredients would normally be increased for twice the amount of wine being made it stands to reason that if three gallons are being made the amount of each ingredient must be increased three times and so on. But you would be surprised at the number of people who have written from time to time asking whether *all* ingredients must be doubled or trebled according to the amount of wine being made. Adding acid and tannin is not necessary in all cases – notably where fresh fruits from hedgerow and garden are being used – as these contain enough in themselves. But the materials we are using to make the wines in this chapter lack both – except the apricots and peaches which contain enough acid, but as we are using so little in each recipe, there would not be enough acid for a good ferment or a good wine.

The tea and acid in these recipes – acid in the form of lemon juice – are essentials for a good fermentation and a round fully-flavoured wine. In certain recipes only a little acid is added; this is because the fruit being used contains some but not enough. The tea is used to obtain the tannin it contains. Those with experience in using grape tannin may use this in the amount required according to their experience. I recommend tea as this is a cheap and convenient source. The tea should be freshly made – about 1 teaspoonful to half-pint water. This should be allowed to stand covered for five minutes and then strained free of leaves before being added to the must.

Lemon juice is a useful source of citric acid. Where it is more convenient a quarter ounce of citric acid may be used instead of two lemons. Where larger amounts of wine are being made the amount of acid and tannin must be increased proportionately e.g. twice the amount of tea and acid (or lemon juice).

VERMOUTH

French style is sweeter – 3 lb. sugar as given in recipe. For Italian style which is drier use 2½ lb.

2 lb. potatoes · 1 orange · 2 lemons
2 fl. oz. Vermouth extract · 3 lb. sugar
¼ pint strong tea · all-purpose yeast · nutrient
and approx. 1 gallon water

Do not peel potatoes, but scrub them thoroughly and slice finely or grate them. Boil in half-gallon water for ten minutes (or until water becomes clear). Put half sugar to be used in fermenting pail, strain boiling potatoes onto this. Discard potatoes. Stir until sugar is dissolved and then make up to roughly ¾ gal. with boiling water. Add tea, lemon and orange juice (no pips), cover as directed and leave until cool. Add extract and yeast, cover again and leave until cool. Add extract and yeast, cover again and leave until vigorous ferment dies down – about 5-6 days. Boil remaining sugar in 1 pint water for 2-3 minutes. Allow to cool and add this to rest. Add nutrient, cover again, leaving thus for a further 3-4 days. After this, transfer to gallon jar leaving as much deposit behind as you can. Fill the jar with boiled cooled water to the beginning of neck. Fit fermentation lock and leave until all fermentation has ceased.

VERMOUTH – USING RAISINS

See notes 'Sweet or Dry' on page 49.

1 lb. raisins · 2 lemons · ¼ pint strong tea
2 fl. oz. Vermouth extract · 2 lb. sugar
all-purpose yeast nutrient · approx. 1 gal. water

Put raisins in fermenting vessel. Boil half the sugar to be used in half gallon of water for 2-3 minutes and pour over the raisins. Add lemon juice and tea and allow liquor to cool. Add extract and yeast. Cover as directed and leave for five days. If raisins rise to surface, push them under once a day and cover again at once.

Strain out raisins, squeezing well but not too hard. Return strained liquor to cleaned fermenting vessel. Boil remaining sugar in quart water for 2-3 minutes. Allow this to cool and add to the rest. Cover again and allow to ferment on for a further five days.

After this, add nutrient, transfer to gallon jar, leaving as much deposit behind as you can and fill to beginning of neck with boiled cooled water. Fit fermentation lock and leave until all fermentation has ceased.

VERMOUTH USING PARSNIPS AS A BASE

Those of you who know they make good wines from parsnips may prefer to use these instead of potatoes when making Vermouth. In this event, substitute 2 lb. of parsnips for the 2 lb. of potatoes given in the first recipe. Prepare parsnips as for potatoes and then carry on as if you were using potatoes.

SLOE GIN WINE

1 lb. raisins (or dates) · 2 fl. oz. sloe gin extract
2 lemons · 2½ lb. sugar · yeast · nutrient
approx. 1 gal. water · ¼ pint tea
as directed on p. 90

Boil half the sugar in 3 quarts water for 2-3 minutes making sure all is dissolved and while boiling pour over raisins in fermenting vessel. Allow to cool, add strained juice of lemons, tea, extract, yeast and nutrient. Cover as directed and ferment in warm place for 5-6 days.

Strain out raisins, squeeze well and return strained wine to cleaned fermenting vessel. Cover as before and leave to ferment 3-4 more days. Then pour gently into gallon jar, leaving as much deposit behind as you can. Boil remaining sugar in 1 pint water and, when cool, add to jar. Fill jar to where neck begins with boiled cooled water, fit fermentation lock and leave in warm place until all fermentation has ceased.

PRUNELLE WINE

½ lb. dried prunes · 1 fl. oz. prunelle extract
juice 2 lemons · 3 lb. sugar · yeast · nutrient
approx. 1 gal. water · ¼ pint tea
as directed on p. 90

Boil half the sugar in 3 quarts water for 2-3 minutes making sure all sugar is dissolved and pour over prunes while boiling. Allow to cool, add extract, tea, strained lemon juice, yeast and nutrient.

Cover as directed and leave to ferment for 5-6 days. Crush prunes by hand after two days and cover again at once.

After 5-6 days, strain, squeeze a little and put strained wine into cleaned fermenting vessel. Leave covered as before to ferment for further 3-4 days.

Then pour carefully into gallon jar leaving as much deposit behind as you can. Boil remaining sugar in 1 pint water for 2-3 minutes making sure all is dissolved and when cool put this into the jar.

Fill to where neck begins with boiled cooled water, fit fermentation lock and leave to ferment in warm place until all fermentation has ceased.

CREAM OF APRICOT WINE

1 lb. apricots · ½ fl. oz. cream of apricot extract
3 lb. sugar · juice 1 lemon · yeast · nutrient
approx. 1 gal. water · ¼ pint tea
as directed on p. 90.

Halve apricots and remove stones. Put them in fermenting vessel. Boil half the sugar in 3 quarts water for 2-3 minutes making sure all sugar is dissolved and while still boiling pour over the fruit in the fermenting vessel.

Allow to cool, add extract, strained lemon juice, tea, yeast and nutrient. Cover as directed and leave to ferment in warm place for 5-6 days. Crush fruits by hand once during that time and cover again at once.

Strain out solids, squeeze a little and return strained wine to cleaned fermenting vessel. Cover as before and leave to ferment a further 3-4 days. Then pour wine carefully into gallon jar, leaving as much deposit behind as you can. Boil remaining sugar in 1 pint water for 2-3 minutes making sure all sugar is dissolved and when cool pour into the rest. Fill jar to where neck begins with boiled cooled water, fit fermentation lock and leave in warm place until all fermentation has ceased.

CREAM OF PEACH WINE

1 lb. peaches · ½ fl. oz. cream of peach extract
3 lb. sugar · juice 1 lemon · yeast . nutrient
approx. 1 gal. water · tea as directed on p. 90

Remove skin from peaches, stone and quarter them

and put into fermenting vessel. Boil half the sugar in 3 quarts water for 2-3 minutes making sure all sugar is dissolved and while still boiling pour over peaches. Allow to cool, add extract, tea, strained lemon juice, yeast and nutrient. Cover as directed and leave to ferment in warm place for 5-6 days. Crush fruits by hand once during this time and cover again at once.

Strain, squeeze well and return strained wine to cleaned fermenting vessel. Leave covered as before in warm place to ferment for 2-3 more days. Then pour gently into gallon jar, leaving as much deposit behind as you can.

Boil remaining sugar in 1 pint water for 2-3 minutes and when cool add to rest. Fill jar to where neck begins with boiled cool water, fit fermentation lock and leave in warm place until all fermentation has ceased.

RATAFIA WINE

1 lb. raisins or dates · 2 fl. oz. Ratafia extract
2½ lb. sugar · juice 2 lemons · yeast · nutrient
approx. 1 gal. water · tea as directed on p. 90

Boil half the sugar in 3 quarts water for 2-3 minutes making sure all sugar is dissolved and pour over raisins in fermenting vessel while still boiling. Allow to cool, add extract, strained lemon juice, tea, yeast nutrient, and ferment in warm place, covered as directed for 5-6 days. Crush raisins by hand once during that time and cover again at once.

Strain out solids, squeeze well and return strained wine to cleaned fermenting vessel. Leave covered as before in warm place to ferment for further 3-4 days.

Then pour carefully into gallon jar leaving as much deposit behind as you can.

Boil remaining sugar in 1 pint water for 2-3 minutes and when cool add to rest. Fill jar to where neck begins with boiled cooled water, fit fermentation lock and leave in warm place until all fermentation has ceased.

MIRABELLE WINE

2 lb. carrots · 2 lemons · 3 lb. sugar
2 fl. oz. Mirabelle extract · yeast · nutrient
approx. 1 gal. water · tea as directed on p. 90

Do not peel carrots, but scrub them thoroughly and grate them. Boil them for ten minutes in 3 quarts water.

Put half the sugar in fermenting vessel and strain boiling carrot water onto this. Stir until all sugar is dissolved. Discard carrots.

Allow to cool, add extract, strained lemon juice, tea, yeast, nutrient and ferment in warm place covered as directed for 5-6 days.

Then pour carefully into gallon jar leaving as much deposit behind as you can.

Boil remaining sugar in 1 pint water for 2-3 minutes and when cool add to rest. Fill to where neck of jar begins with boiled cooled water, fit fermentation lock and leave until all fermentation has ceased. *Note.* There may be no necessity to add water at the final stage so do not worry if there is not enough space for this.

REVERENDINE WINE
RED CURAÇAO WINE · MANDARINE WINE

There is no need to give full details for making these wines because the recipe for Mirabelle wine (above) is quite suitable. Merely follow the recipe, but instead of using Mirabelle extract, use either Reverendine, or Red Curaçao, or Mandarine, according to your choice.

WHITE CURAÇAO WINE

This recipe is suitable for use with all the extracts listed here – White Curaçao, Kummel, Danzig, Marasquin, Yellow Convent, Green Convent and Eau-de-Vie.

Merely follow the recipe below using either of the above extracts according to your choice. In most, the colour of the resulting wine will be as near identical to the colour of the liqueur, but in others it will not be identical – though there will only be a slight difference.

1 lb. sultanas · 2 fl. oz. of extract of your choice (see above) · 2½ lb. sugar · juice 1 lemon · yeast nutrient · approx. 1 gal. water

Boil half the sugar to be used in 3 quarts water for 2 minutes and pour over the sultanas in the fermenting vessel.

Allow to cool, add extract of your choice, the strained lemon juice, yeast and nutrient and ferment covered as directed for 5-6 days. Crush sultanas by hand once or twice during this time and cover again at once.

Strain out solids, squeeze well, and return strained wine to cleaned fermenting vessel to ferment for further 3-4 days.

Then pour carefully into gallon jar leaving as much heavy deposit behind as you can.

Boil remaining sugar in 1 pint water for 2 minutes and when cool add to rest. If space is left, fill jar to where neck begins with boiled cooled water. Fit fermentation lock and leave until all fermentation has ceased.

CHERRY BRANDY WINE

$\frac{1}{2}$ lb. dried elderberries · 4 drops almond essence
2 fl. oz. Cherry Brandy extract · juice 2 lemons
$\frac{1}{4}$ pint of freshly made strong tea · yeast · nutrient
approx. 1 gal. water · 3 lb. sugar

Wash elderberries thoroughly in several lots of water and let them drain. Put them in fermenting vessel.

Boil half sugar to be used in 3 quarts water for 2 minutes and pour while boiling over the elderberries. Allow to cool, add extract, tea, lemon juice, yeast and nutrient and allow to ferment covered as directed for 6-7 days. Crush berries by hand once or twice during this time and cover again at once.

Strain out solids, squeeze well, and return strained wine to cleaned fermenting vessel to ferment for further 3-4 days.

Then pour carefully into gallon jar leaving as much heavy deposit behind as you can.

Boil remaining sugar in 1 pint water for 2 minutes and when cool add to the rest, together with the almond essence. If space is left, fill to where neck begins with boiled cooled water. Fit fermentation lock and leave until all fermentation has ceased.

Special Note on Use of T'Noirot Extracts

It is a fact that many of you will have a good deal of experience in wine-making before reading this book and many of you will have developed some skill in making certain types of wines well and consistently where others simply cannot make a good wine with the same ingredients. Odd as this is, I encounter it all along the line. At wine-making clubs, and such like, and at other places I visit where home-made wines are discussed, I am often asked for an explanation. No one could be conclusive about this. Indeed, anybody who tried would be merely kidding you in the hope of making you think he knows a lot about wine-making. Such people can be a confounded nuisance because they merely mislead where help is genuinely needed.

Many factors bear on the result of a finished wine, and it is not my intention to discuss them here because I have done this in other books. So let me concern myself with those people who know in advance that they *always* turn out a top-rate wine with say, potatoes, or maybe it's parsnips or carrots.

But whatever it is they use and make good wines with, they should consider the possibility of making those wines with half the ingredients for use with T'Noirot extracts.

I am suggesting this because some people simply cannot make a good wine with a certain ingredient. For example, I make good orange wine – always have done – but my neighbour always makes his better, yet he uses the same oranges, yeast, sugar, water, nutrient, and what is more, I showed him how to make wine. Similarly, his elderberry wine is never a touch upon mine, yet we gather the fruits together, use the same amounts, the same water, yeast, sugar and nutrient. This, I think is the main reason for their being so many recipes for each sort of wine. Operators failing one way try another and another failing with this tries something different. And in no time at all, ten to twenty recipes are available where there was merely one.

So all you wine-makers of experience in making top-rate wines, take my tip and work anyway you want bearing in mind that you must not produce a wine with a flavour of its own and one difficult to mask. If you will read through the notes at the head of this chapter once again you will understand more clearly what I mean.

If you do this, I am certain you will learn to make wines to surpass your wildest hopes. But do bear in mind that the colour of the finished wine should be the colour of the extract in its diluted state.

17

Wines from Dried Fruit Alone and with Synthetic Must

Whatever may be said – and it is a good deal – for making wines from fresh fruit from garden and hedgerow and from concentrated grape juice, which is the same as used by the great commercial concerns who turn out some of the finest wines in the world, there is a good deal more to be said for making wines from dried fruit. In fact, I understand from one dealer in home wine equipment that making wines from dried fruit is banned in Germany because the wines are of such excellence, and if allowed to be made, a vast industry might suffer greatly – Germany being a wine-growing and wine-making country on a par with France.

But we have no such restrictions. Years ago I made dried-fruit wines only during winter when fresh fruits were not available. But I make them now as a matter of course, not only because of shortage of fresh fruits, but because they are such excellent wines the ingredients for which are readily obtainable.

101

Another factor making these ingredients most popular is that there is far less work in their preparation for the fermenting vessel. Far less than the normal amount of fruit is needed; this is because 1 lb. of dried fruit represents roughly 4 lb. of fresh fruit. Thus 1 lb. raisins represents roughly 4 lb. grapes, and it is roughly the same with other fruits. Another factor is that most dried fruits contain a lot of sugar, so that less than the usual amount is required.

Dried Fruits and Synthetic Must

Wines made from dried fruits in conjunction with what is known as synthetic must are even better than those made with dried fruits alone.

The Must is known as Dold Kunstmostansatz; this fermented with water, sugar and yeast makes a very excellent light table wine in its own right. But I will discuss this aspect of it later in this chapter.

In all the recipes in this chapter for dried-fruit wines I include the use of synthetic Must, for I have found it invaluable in these. But you can, if you prefer, leave this out and carry on as you would if you were using it.

The Must costs 2/6 per bottle. It is a perfectly balanced Must ready for fermenting and my experience with this has not only gratified me but surprised me a good deal. The wine it makes is a light, fine wine with a fresh flavour, and it improves vastly with age. I have some now five years old and it has turned into a very excellent table wine of some character. The idea of using it with dried fruit was to get more balance in the Must than I could obtain from dried fruits alone, without going to a lot of trouble to balance acid and tannin and other matter. And, as most of my ideas do, this worked extremely well. I found that while dried fruits alone make top-rate wines, the synthetic Must added freshness of flavour that made them even better.

The Must alone will make two gallons of very light wine, but I found this a little too light for my liking, so I used the amount required for two gallons to make one. This was sharp and rough when fermentation ceased, but after a year was really delightful; the sharpness having become a pleasant freshness and harshness gone altogether.

When using the Must alone it may be made – as other wines – sweet, medium or dry. But when made sweet I found it lacked flavour. Therefore, it would be better to make it dry to medium-sweet. See recipes for using Must only on p. 105.

The facts emerging from my experiments with this Must and dried fruits were that we have two ways of using them. First, we can use a little dried fruit to improve wines made with the Must, and we can use a little Must to improve wines made with dried fruit. In one we use less Must and more fruit, while in the other we use more Must and less fruit. We are, as already mentioned, able to use either the Must or dried fruit separately.

It is clear from this that this type of wine-making offers enormous scope for further experiment. Any adventurous wine-maker using common sense will think up all sorts of ideas from the details above. Firstly, you can make wines by the recipes here, and then, after a while, when you know what you are doing and why you are doing it in one particular way, you will think up recipes of your own, try them out in one-gallon lots, and the chances are, be delighted with most of them. Naturally, you will not like them all. But I am willing to wager a bottle of my best that your friends – and you'll be surprised how many you have when there's a stock of wine under the stairs – will be amazed that you made them yourself. The delightful part about this is that while you will make one wine you don't like, to every one you do to start with, your friends will like best the one you don't like at all. This means that you can rid yourself of the wine you do not like yourself while pleasing your friends and at the same time keep the best for yourself.

This, I think, is the nearest you will ever get to 'having it both ways'.

SPECIAL NOTE ON DRIED FRUITS

Letters often reach me from people who cannot obtain dried fruits sold loosely – that is weighed at the shop counter. They ask if the pre-packed polythene wrapped or boxed product is as good as those they are used to and if they are suitable for wine-making.

Pre-packing is here to stay if only from the time-saving factor. The product inside is as good – better in fact. Packed in this way the fruit remains fresher and are cleaned before packed and are kept clean all through, whereas the fruits sold loosely often had lost some of their quality and, owing to being left about uncovered for perhaps weeks on end, by this time had picked up no end of dust.

The packeted stuff is the best to use.

Lemons. It will be seen in the recipes that I advise the juice of lemons. This is to add acid – an essential of wines and an essential of good fermentation. Those who prefer to use citric acid from a chemist – this is very cheap – may do so, but bear in mind that 1 oz. citric acid is represented by approximately eight medium-sized lemons. Therefore, to replace the juice of two lemons given in a recipe one would need to add a quarter ounce of citric acid – about 3d.

RECIPE FOR USING SYNTHETIC MUST – ALONE

As mentioned, I found when using one bottle of the Must to make two gallons of wine according to the producer's instructions, the wine was a little too light for my liking. This may be a fault of mine because I like slightly stronger than average flavours.

Therefore, I suggest you make an experimental lot of one gallon as follows and keep it for one year after fermentation has ceased. If it is a little too light for you, a little more of the Must may be added. Because this will be so little, the alcohol content will not be reduced. On the other hand if it is too strongly flavoured – but I doubt this possibility – you may reduce the amount of Must used next time.

As this wine is so cheap to make – 5/- per gallon (10d per bottle), including cost of sugar – it will not be a calamity if the first batch does not come up to expectations.

In any case, if this first batch did happen to be too strongly flavoured after one year's keeping, you would find it had mellowed a good deal after a couple of years.

If you cannot wait that long, the simple answer is blend it with another wine (see Blending, p. 65).

LIGHT TABLE WINE

$\frac{3}{4}$ bottle synthetic Must · $2\frac{1}{2}$ lb. sugar for dry wine
3 lb. for medium · yeast · nutrient
approx. 1 gal. water

Boil half the sugar in 3 quarts water for 2-3 minutes stirring until all is dissolved. Allow to cool, pour into fermenting vessel, add the Must, nutrient and yeast. Cover as directed and ferment in warm place for 7-8 days.

Then transfer to gallon jar leaving as much deposit behind as you can. Boil remaining sugar in 1 pint water for 2-3 minutes and when thoroughly cooled, add to the jar. Fill jar to where neck begins with boiled cooled water if necessary.

Fit fermentation lock and leave until all fermentation has ceased.

Earlier in this chapter I mentioned that you can leave out the Must and carry on making the wines from dried fruit as if you were using the Must. This does not apply to the recipes immediately following. This is because so little dried fruit is being used that the resulting wines would not be nearly so good if the Must is not included. In other words, not enough dried fruit is being used to make a good wine in its own right. Therefore, the Must is essential here. It is in the recipes which begin on page 112 that the Must may be left out if you prefer.

So that mistakes do not occur, the recipes are numbered. For example all recipes requiring the Must are numbered as Dried Prune Wine (or whatever it might be) No. 1. The recipes designated No. 2 are the recipes where the Must may be left out if you prefer.

DRIED PRUNE WINE NO. 1

1 lb. dried prunes · juice 1 lemon
½ bottle synthetic Must · yeast · nutrient
approx. 1 gal. water
Sugar: 2¼ lb. for dry wine · 2¾ lb. for medium
3 lb. for sweet

Cut up the prunes, leaving stones in, and put into fermenting vessel. Boil half the sugar in 3 quarts water for 2-3 minutes and pour while boiling over the prunes. Add strained lemon juice, and allow mixture to cool well. Then add yeast and nutrient and synthetic Must.

Cover as directed and leave to ferment for 7-8 days. Strain out solids and put strained wine into gallon jar. Boil remaining sugar in 1 pint water and add this when cool to the jar. Then fill to where neck begins with boiled cooled water, fit fermentation lock and leave until all fermentation has ceased.

RAISIN WINE NO. 1

1 lb. raisins · juice 1 lemon · ½ bottle synthetic Must
yeast · nutrient · approx. 1 gal. water
Sugar: 2 lb. for dry wine · 2½ lb. for medium
2¾ lb. for sweet wine

Boil half the sugar in 3 quarts water for 2-3 minutes and pour while boiling over whole raisins in fermenting vessel. Add strained juice of lemon and allow mixture to cool well. Then add yeast, nutrient and synthetic Must.

Cover as directed and leave to ferment for 7-8 days. Each day, squeeze raisins by hand and cover again at once.

After 7-8 days, strain out raisins and squeeze and put strained wine into gallon jar leaving as much deposit behind as you can.

Boil remaining sugar in 1 pint water for 2-3 minutes and when cool pour into jar. Then fill to where neck begins with boiled cooled water, fit fermentation lock and leave until all fermentation has ceased.

SULTANA WINE No. 1

This makes an excellent imitation of Sauternes. Proceed in exactly the same way as for Raisin Wine No. 1 – the preceding recipe – using the same amount of ingredients but substituting 1 lb. sultanas for 1 lb. raisins.

DRIED APRICOT WINE No. 1

1 lb. dried apricots · (no lemon)
½ bottle synthetic Must · yeast · nutrient
approx. 1 gal. water
Sugar: 2½ lb. for dry wine · 2¾ lb. for medium
3 lb. for sweet wine

Wash and cut up apricots. Boil half the sugar in 3 quarts water for 2-3 minutes and pour while boiling over cut-up fruit in fermenting vessel. Allow to cool well, add synthetic Must, yeast and nutrient. Cover as directed and leave to ferment for 7-8 days. Squeeze the fruit and stir every other day, covering again at once.

After 7-8 days, strain out solids, and put strained wine into gallon jar leaving as much deposit behind as you can.

Boil remaining sugar in 1 quart water for 2-3 minutes and when cool add this to jar. Then fill to where neck begins with boiled cooled water, fit fermentation lock and leave until all fermentation has ceased.

DRIED PEACH WINE NO. 1

Proceed in exactly the same way as for Dried Apricot Wine No. 1 using the same amounts of ingredients but substituting 1 lb. dried peaches for 1 lb. dried apricots.

DRIED BILBERRY WINE NO. 1
(An excellent claret when made dry)

½ lb. dried bilberries · ½ bottle synthetic Must
Yeast · nutrient · juice of half a lemon
Sugar: 2½ lb. for dry wine · 2¾ lb. for medium
3¼ lb. for sweet wine · approx. 1 gal. water

Wash bilberries thoroughly in several lots of water and let them drain. Put them in fermenting vessel.

Boil half the sugar in 3 quarts water for 2-3 minutes and pour while boiling over the fruits. Add strained lemon juice and allow mixture to cool well. Add the Must, yeast and nutrient. Cover as directed and ferment for 5-6 days.

Then strain out solids and put strained wine into gallon jar. Boil remaining sugar in 1 pint water for 2-3 minutes and when cool add to jar. Then fill to where neck begins with boiled cooled water if necessary. Fit fermentation lock and leave until all fermentation has ceased.

DRIED ELDERBERRY WINE NO. 1
(An excellent claret when made dry)

½ lb. dried elderberries · ½ bottle synthetic Must
juice 1 lemon · yeast · nutrient · approx. 1 gal. water
Sugar: $2\frac{1}{4}$ lb. for dry wine · $2\frac{3}{4}$ lb. for medium
$3\frac{1}{4}$ lb. for sweet

Wash berries in several lots of water, let drain for a minute or two. Put them in fermenting vessel. Boil half sugar in 3 quarts water for 2-3 minutes and pour while boiling over the fruits. Add strained lemon juice and allow mixture to cool well. Add Must, yeast and nutrient. Cover as directed and leave to ferment for 5-6 days.

Then strain out solids and put strained wine into gallon jar. Boil remaining sugar in 1 pint water for 2-3 minutes and when cool add to jar. Then fill to where neck begins with boiled cooled water if space is left. Fit fermentation lock and leave until all fermentation has ceased.

DRIED CURRANT WINE No. 1
*(Makes an excellent claret but often **best** when medium sweet)*

¾ lb. dried currants · ½ bottle synthetic Must
juice 1 lemon · yeast · nutrient · approx. 1 **gal.** water
Sugar: 2 lb. for dry wine · 2½ lb. **for** medium
3 lb. for sweet wine

Put currants in fermenting vessel. **Boil** half the sugar in 3 quarts water for 2-3 minutes and while boiling pour over the currants. Add lemon juice and synthetic Must and allow to cool. When well cooled add yeast and nutrient and cover as directed and leave to ferment for 7-8 days. Each day squeeze currants by hand and cover again at once.

Then strain out solids, put strained wine into gallon jar leaving as much deposit behind as you can. Boil remaining sugar in 1 pint water for 2-3 minutes and when cool add to jar. Then fill to where neck begins if space is left. Fit fermentation lock and leave until all fermentation has ceased.

As mentioned earlier in this chapter, recipes designated as No. 2 are those in which the synthetic Must may be left out. This is because sufficient dried fruit is being used to make good wine in its own right.

If you leave. out the synthetic Must, you should add a quarter pint of strong tea and the juice of one lemon in addition to that given in the recipes.

Those with experience will know at once what they want to do, those without it should stick to the recipes to start with.

The wines in this section are of a heavier nature; fuller-bodied and with a heavier bouquet. They are better made medium sweet to sweet rather than dry as a dry wine is better for having less flavour. Those designated No. 1 are better as dry wines than these would be owing to there being less strength of flavour of the ingredient. You would not like these fuller-flavoured wines when bone dry because when they *are* bone dry, their strength of flavour becomes more marked.

Those who know they must have all wines bone dry – strength of flavour or otherwise – may make them dry merely by using the amount of sugar given in the recipes. Sugar required in these recipes is less than in the other dried fruit recipes because we are using more fruit, and this, as I have already mentioned, contains roughly 50% sugar. The exceptions are dried elderberries and dried bilberries which contain very little sugar.

It is often found that a very heavy deposit forms in these wines and that they sometimes take a little longer than usual to clear. Neither of these points need bother you unduly, simply because they are quite natural occurrences, but someone was sure to write to me about this and I hope this note will forestall them.

DRIED PRUNE WINE No. 2
(*A burgundy – port style*)

2 lbs. dried prunes · juice 2 lemons · yeast · nutrient
approx. 1 gal. water. Sugar: 2 lb. for dry wine
$2\frac{1}{2}$ lb. for medium · 3 lb. for sweet
$\frac{1}{2}$ bottle synthetic Must

Soak prunes overnight in just enough water to cover. When swollen to normal size add just enough water so that they are covered again and simmer gently for three minutes.

Put half the sugar in fermenting vessel and pour over this the simmering prunes and juice. Stir until all sugar is dissolved and allow to cool. Add strained lemon juice and synthetic Must and allow to cool. Add yeast and nutrient, cover as directed and leave to ferment for 6-7 days. During this time break up the prunes by hand and cover again at once.

Then strain out solids, press well by hand and put strained wine into gallon jar. Boil remaining sugar in 1 pint of water for 2-3 minutes and when cool add to jar. If space is left, fill jar to where neck begins with boiled cooled water, fit fermentation lock and leave until all fermentation has ceased.

Raisin Wine No. 2

5 lb. raisins · juice 2 lemons · yeast · nutrient
$\frac{1}{2}$ bottle synthetic Must · approx. 1 gal. water
Sugar: add no sugar if dry wine required · add
$\frac{1}{4}$ lb. for medium · $\frac{3}{4}$ lb. for sweet

Mince raisins and put them in fermenting vessel. Boil sugar if being used (if not, water only) in 3 quarts water for 2-3 minutes and pour while boiling over the raisins. Add lemon juice and synthetic Must and allow mixture to cool. Add yeast and nutrient, cover as directed and leave to ferment for 7-8 days. Stir once or twice during this time and cover again at once.

HWM

Strain out solids, wring out fairly hard by hand and put strained wine into gallon jar. Fill to where neck begins with boiled cooled water, fit fermentation lock and leave until all fermentation has ceased.

SULTANA WINE NO. 2

6 lb. sultanas · juice 1 lemon · yeast · nutrient
½ bottle synthetic Must · approx. 1 gal. water
Sugar: sultanas contain less sugar than raisins
use ½ lb. for dry wine · ¾ lb. for medium
1 lb. for sweet wine

Proceed in exactly the same way as for Raisin Wine Recipe No. 2.

DRIED APRICOT WINE NO. 2

2 lb. dried apricots · no lemon · ½ bottle synthetic
Must · yeast · nutrient · approx. 1 gal. water
Sugar: 2 lb. for dry wine · 2½ lb. for medium
3 lb. for sweet

Wash and cut up or mince apricots and put them in fermenting vessel.

Boil half the sugar in 3 quarts water for 2-3 minutes and pour while boiling over apricots. Allow to cool, add synthetic Must, yeast and nutrient. Cover as directed and leave to ferment for 6-7 days. During this time give a good stirring once or twice and cover again at once.

Strain out solids, press well by hand, but do not wring out dry. Put strained wine into gallon jar leaving as much deposit behind as you can. Boil remaining sugar in 1 pint water for 2-3 minutes and when cool add to jar. If space allows, fill to where neck begins with boiled cooled water. Fit fermentation lock and leave until all fermentation has ceased.

DRIED PEACH WINE NO. 2

Proceed in exactly the same way as for Dried Apricot Wine No. 2 using the same amounts of ingredients but substituting dried peaches for dried apricots.

DRIED BILBERRY WINE NO. 2

A top-quality red wine heavier than recipe No. 1 and better made medium sweet to sweet rather than dry.

1 lb. dried bilberries · 1 lb. raisins · juice 1 lemon
½ bottle synthetic Must · yeast · nutrient
Sugar: 2 lb. for dry wine · 2½ lb. for medium
3 lb. for sweet

Wash bilberries in several lots of water and let them drain. Put them into fermenting vessel with chopped or minced raisins.

Boil half the sugar in 3 quarts water for 2-3 minutes and pour while boiling over the fruits. Add strained lemon juice and synthetic Must. Allow to cool. Add yeast and nutrient. Cover as directed and leave to ferment for 5-6 days. During this time give good stirring once or twice and cover again at once. Strain out solids and put strained wine into gallon jar. Boil remaining sugar in 1 pint water for 2-3 minutes and when cool, add to jar. If space allows, fill jar to where neck begins with boiled cooled water. Fit fermentation lock and leave until all fermentation has ceased.

DRIED ELDERBERRY WINE No. 2

A top-quality red wine, heavier than recipe No. 1 and better made medium sweet to sweet rather than dry.

1 lb. dried elderberries · 1 lb. raisins
½ bottle synthetic Must · juice 1 lemon · yeast
nutrient · approx. 1 gal. water
Sugar: 2 lb. for dry wine · 2½ lb. for medium
3 lb. for sweet

Wash elderberries thoroughly in several lots of water and let them drain a minute or two. Put into fermenting vessel with chopped or minced raisins. Boil half the sugar in 3 quarts water for 2-3 minutes and pour while boiling over the fruits. Allow to cool, add strained lemon juice and synthetic Must, mix well and add yeast and nutrient. Cover as directed and leave to ferment for 5-6 days. Stir once or twice during this time and cover again at once.

Strain out solids and put strained wine into

gallon jar. Boil remaining sugar in 1 pint water for 2-3 minutes and when cool add to the rest. Then, if space allows, fill to where neck of jar begins with boiled cooled water. Fit fermentation lock and leave until all fermentation has ceased.

DRIED CURRANT WINE NO. 2

2½ lb. dried currants · ½ bottle synthetic Must
juice 2 lemons · yeast · nutrient · approx 1 gal. water
Sugar: 1 lb. for dry wine · 1½ lb. for medium
2 lb. for sweet wine

Put currants in fermenting vessel. Boil half the sugar in 3 quarts water for 2-3 minutes and while boiling pour over the fruit. Allow to cool, add strained lemon juice and synthetic Must. Give good stirring and add yeast and nutrient.

Cover as directed and leave to ferment for 6-7 days. During this time crush currants by hand once or twice and cover again at once.

Then strain out solids and press well by hand. Put strained wine into gallon jar leaving as much deposit behind as you can.

Boil remaining sugar in 1 pint water for 2-3 minutes and when cool add to jar. If space is left fill to where neck begins with boiled cooled water. Fit fermentation lock and leave until all fermentation has ceased.

18

Synthetic Must and T'Noirot Extract

Those with some time to spare preparing fruit and roots for use with T'Noirot extracts will find their wines a little cheaper than those here. But those without time will not mind paying a few shillings extra per gallon – they will consider the time saving worth the little extra. The results, as my trials proved, are first-rate.

This must be considered the absolute last word in modern wine-making for here neither fruits nor roots are used, but two materials 'straight from the bottle'.

As already mentioned, the synthetic Must is a balanced Must that makes an excellent wine in its own right. But, as explained earlier, the wine is very light indeed. And because of this it is the ideal medium for using with T'Noirot extracts for we need not worry about the flavour of the synthetic Must altering the flavour of the extract. But when using the Must, we must use a little more extract than if we were using say peaches with a peach extract. This is because we shall not be obtaining any flavour at all from the Must. Therefore, it would be cheaper to use a few peaches or apricots with a peach or apricot extract and not to use peach or apricot extracts at all with synthetic Must.

The whole idea here is to produce without any work at all a basic fermentable material for use with a flavouring. In the flavouring (the extract) we have nothing fermentable. In the Must we have a fermentable material with precious little flavour of its own. Therefore, in combining the two, we have the ideal combination.

And if one of the many vigorous yeasts and good nutrients are used, there is no reason at all for fermentation continuing beyond three months. By this time the wines will be brilliantly clear and although you really ought not to, there is no reason for not using them right away.

My exhortations to keep wines two or three years usually go unheeded, but these, like all others, do improve vastly with age. So I do hope you will keep some of them to improve, for until you have done this, you cannot imagine the vast improvement that does take place.

Keep these wines at a constant temperature during fermentation if you possibly can in order to shorten the fermentation period. The ideal temperature being in the region of 65°f.

When fermentation has ceased, these wines are treated in the same manner as others.

Because the Must gives very little colour into the wine there is no fear of the finished product not being the colour of the liqueur flavour which we are using. For example, Vermouth must be the colour of commercial Vermouth while Green Convent must be green, and so on. The Must will not alter this.

It is unlikely that you will be familiar with all the flavours available unless you are fortunate enough to be able to buy bottles of all the liqueurs – an expensive project. So those not familiar with them all must use those they know.

The following is a list of the extracts I have found suitable for use with the synthetic Must. All are used with the method set out separately on page 121.

> Green Convent
> Yellow Convent
> Danzig
> Red Curaçao
> White Curaçao
> Mirabelle
> Prunelle
> Sloe Gin
> Ratafia
> Marasquin
> Mandarine
> Vermouth – French or Italian

Wines made from the above may be made into liqueurs if you want to. This can prove expensive to the majority, but those who have a 'thing' about liqueurs will not mind this. In any case, the home-produced liqueur will be a good deal cheaper than Tea commercial product (see page 121).

The cost of one gallon of wine made with an extract in conjunction with synthetic Must, bearing in mind that we are using more here than if we were using a root or fruit base, is about 12/6. This is made up as follows:

Extract   8/6
Must   1/3 half bottle
Sugar   1/6 to 2/3 according to wine type
Yeast
Nutrient }   1/3
Tea
Lemon   ____
              12/6 – 2/1 per bottle

The joy of this, besides being so cheap, is the kind of wine being made and that there is practically nothing to do except 'start off' the mixture.

When making Vermouth (worth 17/6 per bottle as against the 2/1 above), it may be made sweet or dry. For dry use $2\frac{1}{2}$ lb. sugar, for medium use 3 lb., for sweet use $3\frac{1}{4}$ to $3\frac{1}{2}$ lb. With all other extracts use 3 lb.

Method
$\frac{1}{2}$ bottle synthetic Must · 1 large bottle of extract of your choice · approx. 1 gal. water · 2 tablespoons freshly made tea · $\frac{1}{8}$ oz. citric acid (or juice 1 lemon) yeast · nutrient · sugar (see above)

Boil half the sugar in 3 quarts water for 2-3 minutes. Pour into fermenting vessel and stir in the Must and extract of your choice. Add tea and lemon juice (or citric acid) and allow to cool well covered.

When cool, add yeast and nutrient. Cover as directed and leave to ferment for 7-8 days. If fermenting very vigorously at this stage leave for a further day or two.

Transfer to a gallon jar leaving most of the heavy deposit behind, fit fermentation lock and leave to ferment for one more week.

Then boil remaining sugar in 1 pint water and when cool add to the jar. If space is left at this stage fill jar to where neck begins with boiled water well cooled. Refit the lock and leave until fermentation has ceased.

Thereafter the wines are treated as directed.

19

Wines from Concentrated Grape Juice and Dried Fruits

At various wine-making clubs where I give talks I am often asked for recipes for using grape concentrate with dried fruits. It seems that even with the excellent results achieved with concentrates, many believe that they can be improved upon.

The object in making wines at home should be to make good wines and to strive to improve their quality so that in the end one has a wine that they can claim could not be better in consideration of the ingredients used. And this happy state of affairs is quite easy to achieve.

And I think that once you have come this far, you should call it a day. I say this because having achieved what years ago would have been regarded as an impossibility, we should be satisfied. But only because this endless striving to improve can result in the opposite. Improve by all means, but if you keep adding ingredients to a basic recipe or keep altering the amounts, you will find that when you have what you thought would be the result, it is

123

nothing like the wine is was or what you hoped it would be. In other words, you have put your foot in it!

I am perfectly serious. Writing as I do about this subject, I am experimenting ceaselessly to find new methods and recipes for good wines, and I do quite often find, on sampling an experiment, that the basic recipe did, after all, make the best wine.

One may well argue that you could not hope to improve upon wines made from concentrated grape juice. That may be so. But using this material as a base as we use the Synthetic Must as a basic ingredient, we are able to make a wider variety of wines from the basic material by using dried fruit.

This is different from trying to improve on wines made from grape juice. We are merely using our heads to make a variety of wines instead of making just one sort. And whether you will agree or not is another matter, but I have found that in many cases I have liked the wines made from the recipes in this chapter more than some made from the concentrate only. But this may be because I am a difficult bloke to please. This is not to suggest that concentrates do not make as good wines as they should. They make absolutely top-class wines, but by using half the normal amount of this with half the usual amount of dried fruit, wines quite different to those turned out by either are the result. And this method, does, incidentally give better results than blending them, despite what I have had to say to the contrary in the section on blending.

In evolving these recipes it was necessary to assume that a quart of concentrate contains two pounds of sugar. So, when using one pint of concentrate to the gallon it is safe to say the gallon contains one pound of sugar. Dried fruits being approximately 50% sugar means that where one pound of this is used it will put half a pound of sugar into the Must. So we merely work out the sugar requirements bearing in mind that it will vary with your requirements, dry, medium or sweet. The amounts of sugar are given in the recipes.

Now, because they are diluting the little acid there is in the concentrate and because the dried fruits contain none, we shall have to add some. But do not fear that the lemon juice or citric acid included in the recipes will flavour the wine of lemons. There is not enough for that. This is necessary for satisfactory yeast action and also to give sufficient acid into the wine without which it would lack flavour to such an extent that it could be quite lifeless.

Dried Elderberry and Grape Concentrate

½ lb. dried elderberries · 1 pint red concentrate
juice 2 lemons (or ¼ oz. citric acid) · Burgundy
yeast or all-purpose nutrient · 7 pints water
Sugar: 1¼ lb. for dry · 1½ lb. for medium
2 lb. for sweet

Wash elderberries thoroughly in several lots of water and let them drain. Put them into fermentation vessel.

Boil half the sugar to be used in six pints water

for two minutes and while boiling, pour over elderberries.

Allow this mixture to cool, shake the grape juice
well and mix with the elderberries. Add lemon
juice (or citric acid), yeast and nutrient and ferment as for other wines for five days. After this,
strain out the berries, but do not squeeze too much.

Put strained wine into gallon jar. Boil remaining sugar with about half pint of water and when
cool add to the rest. If space is left, fill jar to where
neck begins with boiled cooled water. Fit a fermentation lock and leave until all fermentation has
ceased.

Note. If there is not enough space in the jar for
the final sugar addition after the strained wine is
put into it, wait a few days until fermentation has
used up more of the sugar.

DRIED BILBERRY AND GRAPE CONCENTRATE

$\frac{3}{4}$ lb. dried bilberries · 1 pint red grape concentrate
juice two lemons (or $\frac{1}{4}$ oz. citric acid) · Burgundy or
all-purpose yeast · nutrient · approx. seven pints
water · Sugar: $1\frac{1}{4}$ lb. for dry · $1\frac{1}{2}$ lb. for medium
2 lb. for sweet

Wash bilberries thoroughly in several lots of water
and let them drain. Put them into fermenting
vessel.

Boil half the sugar to be used in six pints water
for two minutes and while boiling pour over the
bilberries.

Allow this mixture to cool, then shake the grape juice well and mix with the bilberries. Add lemon juice (or citric acid), yeast and nutrient and ferment for five days.

After this, strain out the berries, but do not squeeze too much.

Put strained wine into gallon jar. Boil remaining sugar in about half pint of water and when cool add to the rest. If space is left, fill jar to where neck begins with boiled cooled water. Fit fermentation lock and leave until all fermentation has ceased. (See note at conclusion of preceding recipe.)

Where raisins, prunes and sultanas are used and these are packeted or wrapped by the producers, there will be no need to wash them. But if these are bought loose, they should be washed as for elderberries.

RAISIN AND GRAPE CONCENTRATE

1 lb. raisins · 1 pint red or white concentrate · juice 2 lemons (or $\frac{1}{4}$ oz. citric acid) · Burgundy or all-purpose yeast · nutrient · approx. 7 pints water
Sugar: $\frac{3}{4}$ lb. for dry · 1 lb. for medium · $1\frac{1}{2}$ lb. for sweet

Put raisins in fermenting vessel. Boil half the sugar to be used in six pints water for two minutes and while boiling pour over the raisins.

Allow mixture to cool, then shake concentrate and mix it well with the raisins.

Add lemon juice (or citric acid), yeast and nutrient and ferment for five days.

After this, strain out the raisins and squeeze as dry as possible. Put strained wine into gallon jar. Boil remaining sugar in about half pint water and, when cool, add to the rest. If space is left, fill to where neck of jar begins with boiled cooled water. Fit fermentation lock and leave to continue until all fermentation has ceased. (See Note at foot of Dried Elderberry and Grape Concentrate recipe.)

PRUNE AND GRAPE CONCENTRATE

1 to $1\frac{1}{2}$ lb. dried prunes · 1 pint red concentrate juice two lemons (or $\frac{1}{4}$ oz. citric acid) · Burgundy or all-purpose yeast · nutrient · approx. 7 pints water · Sugar: $\frac{3}{4}$ lb. for dry · $1\frac{1}{4}$ lb. for medium $1\frac{3}{4}$ lb. for sweet

Open prunes with sharp knife and remove stones. Put prunes in fermenting vessel. Boil half the sugar to be used in six pints water for two minutes and while boiling pour over the prunes.

Allow mixture to cool, shake concentrate and mix well with the prunes. Add lemon juice (or citric acid), yeast and nutrient and ferment for five days.

After this, strain out prunes and wring out as dry as you can. Put strained wine into gallon jar.

Boil remaining sugar in about half pint of water and when cool add to the rest. If space is left in the jar, fill to where neck begins with boiled cooled water. Fit fermentation lock and leave until all fermentation has ceased (see Note at foot of Dried Elderberry and Grape Concentrate recipe).

Sultana and Grape Concentrate

1½ lb. dried sultanas · 1 pint white concentrate
juice two lemons (or ¼ oz. citric acid) · Burgundy
or all-purpose yeast · nutrient · approx. 7 pints
water · Sugar: ¾ lb. for dry · 1¼ lb. for medium
1¾ lb. for sweet

Put sultanas in fermenting vessel. Boil half the
sugar to be used in six pints water for two minutes
and while boiling pour over sultanas.

Allow mixture to cool, shake concentrate and
mix well with sultanas. Add yeast, nutrient and
lemon juice (or citric acid), and ferment for five
days. After this, strain out sultanas and wring out
as dry as you can. Put strained wine into gallon
jar.

Boil remaining sugar in about half pint water
for two minutes and when cool, add to rest. If space
is left in jar, fill to where neck begins with boiled
cooled water. Fit fermentation lock and leave until
all fermentation has ceased (see Note at foot of
Dried Elderberry and Grape Concentrate recipe).

20

Miscellaneous Recipes

Because I have put the following recipes under this heading do not imagine that I mean 'odds and ends recipes'. The reason for putting them under this heading is because there is not enough of each to make a chapter.

The wines these recipes make are absolutely first rate, and to think for a moment that you might be making 'odds and ends' wine would be an insult to the end product.

TEA WINE

There is no doubt that this simple ingredient makes an excellent wine when combined with almost any dried fruit. I have found that prunes give the best results.

It is best to make tea for the purpose rather than save left-overs from the tea-pot.

2 oz. tea · 1 lb. dried prunes · 2 oranges · 2 lemons
all-purpose wine yeast · nutrient · 3 lb. sugar
approx. 7 pints water

Cut prunes down one side with knife and put in fermenting vessel. Boil half sugar to be used in 4 pints water for two minutes and while boiling pour over prunes.

Make tea in usual way allowing to stand for ten minutes. Then strain into jug to keep out tea leaves. Make this up to a quart with boiled water and mix with prunes.

Add juice of strained lemons. Cut up oranges and their peel and float these on the mixture. Allow to cool, add nutrient and yeast and ferment for five days stirring once a day and covering again at once. When stirring squeeze pieces of oranges by hand.

After five days, strain out solids and put strained wine in a gallon jar. Boil remaining sugar in 1 pint water for two minutes and when cool add to rest. If space is left in jar, fill to where neck begins with boiled cooled water, fit fermentation lock and leave until all fermentation has ceased.

I have recommended all-purpose wine yeast for this wine, but I am told by members of wine circles that they obtain very good results with Heath and Heather dried yeast. They use about $\frac{1}{2}$ oz. per gallon.

Orange Wine

The main difference in the many recipes for this wine is in the number of fruits and the use in some recipes of raisins and dates. I find, however, that oranges themselves make a first-rate wine in their own right.

10-14 medium size oranges (or equivalent in larger)
3 lb. sugar · all-purpose yeast · nutrient · about 1
cupful of strong, freshly made strained tea · approx.
7 pints water

Cut up the oranges and their peel fairly small and
put in fermenting vessel. Boil half sugar to be used
in six pints water and pour when cool over the
oranges, the pips of which should be removed when
oranges are cut up.

Add tea, yeast, and nutrient and ferment for five
days during which the oranges should be pressed
by hand once a day and the brew covered again at
once.

After five days, strain out solids, squeeze well and
put strained wine into a gallon jar. Boil remaining sugar in about 1 pint water or less for two
minutes and, when cool, add to the rest. If space is
left in jar, fill to where neck begins with boiled
cooled water, fit fermentation lock and leave until
all fermentation has ceased.

Special note. Oranges are treated with wax and
other materials to prevent the spread of damage
in transit. For this reason it is wise to dip each
orange in boiling water prior to making the wine.
This may be done by pushing each orange under
the surface of the water using a fork and then taking it out and drying with a clean cloth.

ORANGE LIQUEUR

To make some of your orange wine into Liqueur is
quite simple.

There are many Liqueurs with an orange flavour: Grand Marnier and Cointreau are two. And if you sweeten your orange wine to taste and increase the alcohol to 29·2 or 30·5 by volume, you have liqueur of approximately the strength of the commercial product (see Liqueur tables 3 and 4).

DRIED ROSE HIP WINE

An ingredient the Germans claim to be second only to the grape where wine ingredients are concerned.

Rose hips have been used for years for making top-class wines, but like all other wild ingredients they are diminishing rapidly. Very little of the dried product is needed and are obtainable from dealers in home wine ingredients.

12 oz. dried rose hips · juice 2 lemons (or $\frac{1}{4}$ oz. citric acid) · $2\frac{1}{2}$ lb sugar · approx. 1 gal. water · all-purpose yeast · nutrient

Mince rose hips with outer cutting disc removed and put them in fermenting vessel. Add strained juice of lemons or citric acid.

Boil all sugar in 7 pints of water for two minutes and while boiling pour over rose hips. Allow to cool and add yeast and nutrient, and ferment for five days stirring daily and covering again at once.

Strain out solids, put strained wine in gallon jar. If space is left, fill to where neck begins with boiled cooled water, fit fermentation lock and leave until all fermentation has ceased.

ROSE HIP WINE USING ROSE HIP SYRUP

Some time ago a member of a wine-making circle proudly presented me with a bottle of what must have been the first wine made with commercially produced rose hip syrup.

It was a delightful wine; one I have always meant to make but which, alas, owing to constant pressure from other directions, I have not been able to.

Here is the recipe which was given me at the same time as the bottle.

1 pint rose hip syrup · 2½ lb. sugar · Juice 1 lemon juice and rind or rind of 1 orange · all purpose yeast nutrient · approx. 7 pints water · ½ cupful strong tea

Another member of the Circle had produced an excellent wine with this recipe using Heath and Heather dried yeast, ½ oz. per gallon.

Pour the syrup into fermenting vessel. Boil all the sugar in six pints water for two minutes and when off the boil pour into the syrup. Add strained lemon juice and put in the orange cut up small with the peel but no pips.

Allow mixture to cool, add yeast and nutrient and ferment for 7 days. Then strain, put strained wine into a gallon jar and fill to where neck begins with boiled cooled water. Fit fermentation lock and leave until all fermentation has ceased.

BANANA WINE USING FRESH FRUITS

It is only in the past year or so that these ingredients have been used to make wines and I can assure you that the wines they make are very good. These practically unknown recipes will please you.

$3\frac{1}{2}$ lb. bananas weighed after peeling · the skins of 2 bananas · 2 lemons, 2 oranges · $\frac{1}{2}$ lb. raisins · $2\frac{1}{4}$ lb. sugar · $\frac{1}{2}$ cupful fresh tea · all-purpose wine yeast nutrient · approx. 1 gal. water

The bananas should be ripe to the point of being past their best.

Wipe bananas clean with damp cloth. Peel and mash and put them in fermenting vessel. Boil peel of two for two minutes in half pint of water and put strained water with rest. Add chopped raisins and strained juice of lemons. Cut up oranges and their peel and put with rest. Boil half the sugar in 6 pints water for two minutes and while boiling pour over rest of ingredients. Add tea.

Allow to cool, add yeast and nutrient and ferment for ten days. Stir once a day during this time and cover again at once.

After ten days, strain very carefully as there will be a very heavy deposit and we don't want this.

Return strained wine to fermentation vessel for a further deposit to form. Leave to ferment for two more days. Then pour very carefully or siphon into a gallon jar leaving as much deposit behind as you can.

Boil remaining sugar in 1 pint water for two minutes and when cool add to rest. Then fill jar to where neck begins with boiled cooled water if space is left. Fit fermentation lock and leave until all fermentation has ceased.

Note. This wine will look very messy and cloudy during fermentation. But as this slows down the wine will begin to clear.

BANANA AND ROSE HIP WINE USING DRIED INGREDIENTS

14 oz. dried bananas · 6 oz. dried rose hips · juice 2 lemons (or $\frac{1}{4}$ oz. citric acid) · cupful strong freshly-made tea · $2\frac{3}{4}$ lb. sugar · approx. 1 gal. water · all-purpose wine yeast · nutrient

Pour 4 pints cold water on rose hips and dried bananas in bowl. Cover and leave in cool place for twelve hours.

Strain, put bananas and hips in fermenting vessel. Put water ingredients were soaked in into saucepan with 2 more pints water. Stir sugar into this and boil for 2 minutes. While boiling, pour over ingredients in fermentation vessel. Add tea, strained juice of lemons and allow to cool. Then add yeast and nutrient and ferment for five days, stirring daily and covering again at once.

Strain out solids, return strained wine to fermentation vessel and leave to ferment a further five days.

Then pour carefully into a gallon jar leaving as much deposit behind as you can. Fill to where neck begins with boiled cooled water, fit fermentation lock and leave until all fermentation has ceased.

21

Grain Wines

In the mad rush there used to be to imitate commercial wines while using English wild and garden fruits, the use of grains almost died out.

Barley and wheat make two splendid wines. Maize and rice also make two good wines, though I am not fond of the latter two. But if what I see at various wine circles is general, many people like them very much. And since when making wines it is a matter of making what suits you personally, who am I to say which you should make or which you will prefer.

Here I give one basic recipe using wheat. If you want to use barley, or maize, merely substitute these grains working in precisely the same fashion as for wheat. But if you use rice, use 3 lb. instead of 1½ lb. as given for the other grains.

WHEAT WINE

1½ lb. wheat (*or* barley, *or* maize) (If rice 3 lb.) 1 lb. raisins · 2 lemons · 2 oranges · 3 lb sugar · all-purpose wine yeast · nutrient · approx. 1 gal. water
1 cupful freshly-made strong tea

Wash whatever grain you are using in collander under fast-running tap. Then soak overnight in enough water to cover well. Drain off any water left and put grains through a coarse plate of the mincer.

Put this minced material in fermentation vessel with the tea and chopped or minced raisins. Boil half the sugar in 6 pints water for two minutes and while boiling pour over ingredients. Add strained juice of lemons and cut up oranges and peel. Allow to cool, add yeast and nutrient and ferment for ten days, stirring daily and covering again at once.

Strain out solids and return strained wine to fermentation vessel for three days. After this, pour carefully into a gallon jar, leaving as much deposit behind as you can. Boil remaining sugar in 1 pint water for two minutes and when cool add to rest. If space is left, fill to where neck begins with boiled cooled water, fit fermentation lock and leave until all fermentation has ceased.

22

Wines from Ribena

Way back in 1959, I sought the collaboration of V. L. S. Charley Esq., B.Sc., Ph.D., technical director of the Royal Forest factory of the Beecham group and one-time director of the Long Ashton Research station, in making wines from Ribena. Subsequently, I was able to issue recipes for making wine with this famous syrup. The recipes and methods evolved met with the approval of this gentleman.

Since the date mentioned I have carried out further trials and have come to the conclusion that while the recipes evolved all those years ago will give good results today, the one recipe here makes an excellent light to medium table wine.

Bear in mind that one 12 oz. bottle of Ribena contains approximately 7 oz. sugar, the rest being pure undiluted blackcurrant juice of the finest quality.

The syrup is preserved with 350 parts per million S.O.2. but this may be disregarded because we shall not be using enough Ribena to the gallon for this preservative to prevent fermentation. Indeed, the presence of this – which is really the solution produced by dissolving Campden tablets – might well have beneficial effects. The amount of preservative will be reduced greatly by diluting with water.

Two 12 oz. bottles of this syrup made into a one-gallon must as in the recipe will make an excellent light to medium wine of good all round flavour, about five bottles of it.

Bearing in mind that two 12 oz. bottles contain between them 14 oz. of sugar we are able to work in the following manner:

To make a dry wine.

Ribena Wine

2 12 oz. bottles Ribena · 1½ lb. sugar · Burgundy yeast or all-purpose yeast · nutrient · approx. 7 pints water · *No acid*

Boil sugar in 5 pints water for two minutes and when cool pour into Ribena in fermenting vessel.

Add yeast and nutrient. Cover as directed and ferment for eight days. Then transfer to gallon jar leaving as much deposit behind as you can and fill jar to where neck begins with boiled cooled water. Fit fermentation lock and leave until all fermentation has ceased.

Less Dry. For less dry wine use 2 oz. more sugar. Do not make this wine sweet.

If you want a fuller flavoured wine so that it may be made sweet you may use three bottles of Ribena with 1½ lb. sugar working in exactly the same way as already described.

Using Ribena with dried fruits is going to catch

on in a big way once the flavour of the resulting wines has been savoured.

That Ribena itself makes an excellent wine caused me to put on my thinking cap. How little Ribena and how little dried fruit would be needed to make a top-rate wine bearing in mind that the blackcurrant flavour of Ribena would go well with almost any dried fruit giving some flavour of its own? That was the question I asked myself and I came to the conclusion that it would have to be a matter of absolute trial and error. The 'error' aspect being minimised considerably by my many years of experimentation.

Simple and successful recipes were evolved very quickly and I now have pleasure in passing these on to my readers all over the world.

RIBENA AND DRIED PRUNE
(*A burgundy style*)

12 oz. bottle Ribena · 1 lb. dried prunes · Burgundy or all-purpose wine yeast · nutrient · approx. 7 pints water · Sugar: for dry $1\frac{3}{4}$ lb. · for medium 2 lb. · for sweet $2\frac{1}{4}$ to $2\frac{1}{2}$ lb.

Open prunes with knife and put in fermenting vessel.

Boil half sugar to be used in 6 pints water for two minutes and while boiling pour over prunes. Allow to cool, add Ribena, yeast, nutrient and ferment for five days.

Strain out prunes and wring out as dry as you can. Put strained wine in a gallon jar. Boil rest of sugar in 1 pint of water for two minutes and when cool add to rest. If space is left in the jar, fill to where neck begins with boiled cooled water. Fit fermentation lock and leave until all fermentation has ceased.

RIBENA AND DRIED ELDERBERRY
(*A light port style*)

12 oz. bottle Ribena · $\frac{1}{2}$ lb. dried elderberries · Bergundy or all purpose wine yeast · nutrient · approx. 7 pints water · Sugar: for dry 2 lb., for medium $2\frac{1}{4}$ lb., for sweet $2\frac{1}{2}$ to $2\frac{3}{4}$ lb.

Wash elderberries thoroughly in several lots of water and allow to drain.

Boil half the sugar to be used in 6 pints of water and while boiling pour over elderberries in fermenting vessel.

Allow to cool, add Ribena, yeast, nutrient and ferment for five days.

Strain out elderberries and wring out as dry as you can. Put strained wine into a gallon jar. Boil remaining sugar in 1 pint of water for two minutes and when cool add to rest. If space is left in jar, fill to where neck begins with boiled cooled water. Fit fermentation lock and leave until all fermentation has ceased.

RIBENA AND DRIED BILBERRIES

12 oz. bottle Ribena · $\frac{1}{2}$ lb. dried bilberries · Burgundy yeast or all purpose yeast · nutrient · approx. 7 pints water · Sugar: for dry 2 lb. · for medium $2\frac{1}{4}$ lb. · for sweet $2\frac{1}{2}$ to $2\frac{3}{4}$ lb.

Wash bilberries thoroughly in several lots of water and allow to drain. Put them in fermenting vessel.

Boil half the sugar to be used in 6 pints water for two minutes and, while boiling, pour over the bilberries. Allow to cool. Add Ribena, yeast and nutrient and ferment for five days. Strain out bilberries and wring out as dry as you can.

Put strained wine into a gallon jar. Boil rest of sugar in 1 pint water for two minutes and when cool add to rest. If space is left in jar, fill to where neck begins with boiled cooled water.

Fit fermentation lock and leave until all fermentation has ceased.

RIBENA AND RAISIN WINE

12 oz. bottle Ribena · 1 lb. raisins · Burgundy or all-purpose wine yeast · nutrient · approx. 7 pints water · Sugar: for dry $1\frac{1}{2}$ lb. for medium $1\frac{3}{4}$ lb. for sweet 2 to $2\frac{1}{4}$ lb.

Mince or chop raisins and put them in fermenting vessel. Boil half sugar to be used in 6 pints water for two minutes and pour, while boiling, over raisins.

Allow to cool. Add Ribena, yeast and nutrient, and ferment for five days.

Strain out raisins and wring out as dry as you can. Put strained wine into gallon jar. Boil remaining sugar in 1 pint water for two minutes and when cool add to rest. If space is left in jar, fill to where neck begins with boiled cooled water. Fit fermentation lock and leave until all fermentation has ceased.

BLACKCURRANT RUM

Using Ribena wine as a basic material we are able to make the very popular blackcurrant rum.

First make the wine as directed using Ribena Wine recipe and not one of those including dried fruit.

If you will now take a look at Liqueur Table No. 2, you will find that because rum of 70% proof would correspond with Vodka in the table you are able to add 11 oz. of rum to 15 oz. of blackcurrant wine made with Ribena to obtain a standard wine bottle of blackcurrant rum of 25% by volume, or 43.8% proof, which is approximately the strength of commercially produced blackcurrent rum.

If a less strong blackcurrant rum is required, less spirit may be used. It is really just a matter of taste. Some people would want it stronger than others. But by consulting the tables you will see at once how to work out the strength you require.

23

Give your Wines that Professional Touch

There is no doubt that the appearance of many home-made wines is marred by the bottle used and the label – often a bit of gum-strip torn off at random – and a discoloured cork sticking out of the top of the bottle at an angle.

Bottles should be chosen to suit the wines put into them. Light coloured wines should always be put into clear-glass bottles, preferably those with punted bottoms. These are merely transparent bottles with the bottoms pushed up. The idea here is to prevent any slight deposit that may form from being disturbed when the wine is poured. But from the appearance point of view there is nothing to compare with them. Only light, brilliantly clear wines should be put into this type of bottle. Dark red and other dark coloured wines should always be put into dark green or dark brown bottles. These wines put into clear-glass bottles always appear 'muddy'.

The fact that all red and the darker coloured

145

wines are put into dark bottles by the trade should be a guide to amateurs. But it is not just a matter of appearance in the case of the darker wines. It is a fact that red wines often spoil if put into clear-glass bottles. The light penetrating them over long periods has adverse effect upon them.

Having put the wine into decent bottles, use decent corks and a plastic seal to finish off. The flanged cork – shaped similar to a mushroom but flat on top – is ideal. They fit nicely and do not require a cork-screw to remove them. Plastic seals are now obtainable; these are obtainable in tins at about 10/6 per gross. And this, incidentally, is the cheapest way to buy them.

One merely slips the slightly oversize seal over the top of the cork and then presses it down all round. Make sure to press out the little bubble of air which sometimes appears on top of the cork. Having fitted the seal, put the bottle away and in a few hours the seal will have shrunk to form a perfectly airtight seal and a perfect finish to the bottle.

Having come this far, surely it is worth the few pence needed to buy a couple of dozen decent labels.

Many sorts, shapes and sizes and designs are available from dealers in home wine equipment and all one has to do is to write in neatly the type of wine – whether sweet, medium or dry – and the year of making.

If the percentage of alcohol is known, this can also be written in. And if you have added spirit to fortify, the letter 'F' in a corner will remind you of this without letting your friends know that the wine contains added spirit. I mention this because it seems that on no account must an amateur allow a friend to know that the high alcohol content is not just part of his skill in making wines.

If you have merely preserved some wines with Campden tablets, the letter 'P' in one corner will remind you of this.

And do be sure to put the right labels on the bottles otherwise you might have an embarrassment to overcome.

I shall never forget an evening when I had several knowledgeable friends in to a wine and cheese party. I was serving dry elderberry wine – a rarity because elderberries do not normally make good dry wines. Imagine my consternation at the expressions of doubt on the faces of these impressionable friends – friends that I was anxious should be delighted with my wines.

Finding an excuse to forage amongst my considerable cellar, I swept away with an air of dignity and composure, leaving my friends to debate the issue in my absence. On returning from the cellar where I located the mistake I had to admit that the elderberry wine they were enjoying had been made with blackcurrants.

So bottle and label each batch separately.

STRAINING INTO JARS

Many people experience difficulty here. They line a funnel with cloth, pour in fermenting wine containing solids such as raisins only to find that the cloth acts as a lining to the funnel leaving only the small outlet at the bottom for straining. This way, it takes ages and if there are three or four gallons to

do it can take all day. This is because a little has to
be poured into the funnel at a time waiting each
time for straining to take place. Many, therefore,
strain into a bucket and then into the jar. But this
is a bothersome double process.

The idea illustrated in Fig. 1 is an easy answer.
A large funnel is used, this is lined with cloth and
then lifted to about the level shown by the dotted
line. The cloth is then pegged with spring clothes
pegs. Straining several gallons even if there are
several pounds of solids present takes only a few
minutes.

SIPHONING

Siphoning is a part of wine-making, for by this
means we can get all the wine from a jar into bottles
without disturbing the deposit. Whereas, if we
poured it, only half would come over clear because
the deposit would come over too. It is well worth
the little trouble involved to make a decent siphon
as shown in Fig. 2.

The upturned tubing rests on the bottom of the
jar while the open end remains above the deposit.
A two-holed bung is best. This allows for the cen-
tral hole to hold the tube and a second hole to hold
a short piece of glass as an air inlet. I plug this air
inlet with cotton wool as a double safeguard – very
fussy, I am. But best to be safe than sorry, because
if a low alcohol sweet wine is being made a stray
yeast spoor or spoilage yeast could gain access.

Bear in mind that the neck of the jar or bottle to
receive the wine must be on a lower plain than the
bottom of the jar to be emptied.

Put the siphon in place as shown in Fig. 2. Suck

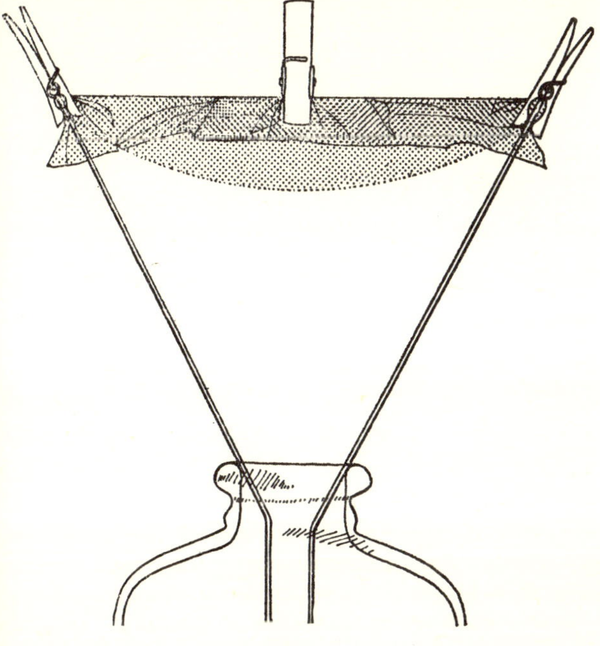

Fig. 1

the other end of the tube until the wine comes, pinch tightly at your lips and then put the end of the tube into the first bottle. When this is full, pinch the end of the tube and put it in the next bottle and allow the wine to flow again. If by accident you break the siphon – that is in this case the flow – you will have to suck again. Carefully done, the tube can be taken from one bottle to the next until the jar is empty.

The deposit and the little wine remaining can

be poured into a spare bottle and used as soon as it has cleared.

The siphon as shown in Fig. 2 can be made for about half a crown. A chemist will supply the glass tubing and bend the end upwards if you ask him nicely for about 1/6. He will also supply a two-holed bung for about 1/-.

FILTERING

I cannot imagine why anybody ever bothers to filter their wines, because if they have been made properly, filtering is the last thing that should be necessary.

Nevertheless, many people do filter using filter papers and then curse everybody except themselves when they find that it takes hours for half a pint to pass through a filter paper. I gave a demonstration of this some time ago and cries of 'oh' and 'ah' greeted the results, simply because I passed a gallon of wine through in three minutes.

The whole art in using these papers is in folding them. If not folded properly, they form a lining to the funnel, leaving only the small outlet under the paper for filtering.

Looking into the funnel the filter paper should appear as shown in Fig. 3.

Bear in mind when filtering that no matter whether papers, asbestos pulp, cotton wool or other media are used, the first pint or so will come through cloudy. This is returned to the funnel. If the second and third pints come over cloudy these should also be returned. It often takes a little time for the wine to run clear.

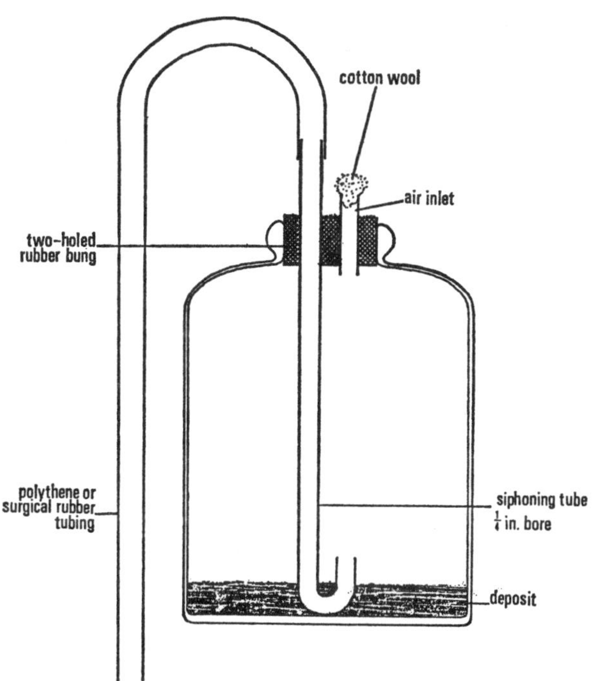

Fig. 2

THAT LIFTED BUNG PROBLEM

Experts will tell you that they are too clever to
have this problem. They claim that they ensure that
fermentation has ceased before they bung down for
keeping. Don't let them kid you along. They may
ensure that fermentation has ceased, but they still
get a bung lift out of the jar sometimes.

Inexperienced wine-makers are apt to put their

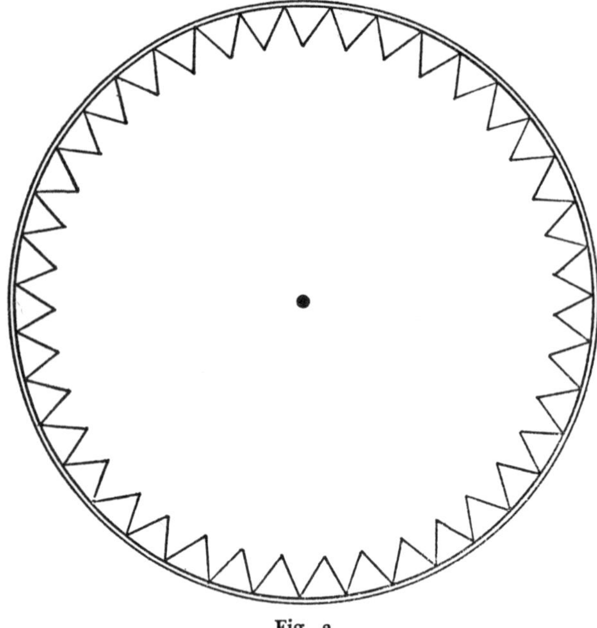

Fig. 3

wines away thinking fermentation has ceased only to find that later on it has re-started and the bung is somewhere around and they go fishing for it. That bung might have been missing for a week or a month leaving the wine exposed to spoilage yeasts and bacteria. A bone-dry wine might not suffer greatly, but what of sweeter wines and those not containing the maximum alcohol? Anything can happen as we have seen under the heading 'Spoiled Wines'.

Another cause of lifted or blown bungs is com-

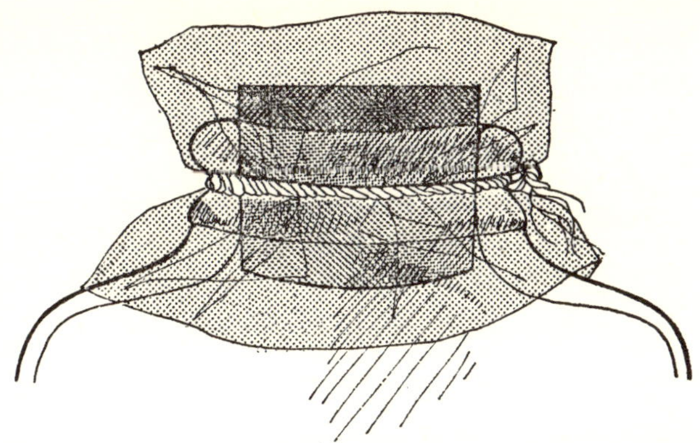

Fig. 4

pression. Jars filled rather full in cold weather tend to blow their bungs owing to warmth of summer expanding the wine. This causes the small amount of air between the wine and the bung to become compressed, and if expansion is great then the bung just goes flying. At best it will pop up to rest on the rim of the jar. Either way, air can be admitted, and for long periods, if daily inspection is not carried out, and I cannot see anybody with all that time on their hands. In any case, they like to put it away and forget it for a year at least if they can. But they do want to be sure it is safe.

The idea shown in Fig. 4 will relieve them of all worry. It is simply a small polythene bag put over the bung and tied tightly with three or four winds of string. The bag is arranged so that the cork can lift if it wants to without bursting through the bag. A piece of strong polythene placed over the bung, lifted and then tied tightly will do just as well provided it leaves space for the bung to lift if it wants to. Wines put away thus protected can be quite forgotten for years if you want to. But if you notice the bung has lifted, you can push it home again without removing the covering. The polythene must not, of course, have any holes in it.

24

Mead

Honey wine. The very idea makes one's mouth water. This is not surprising for honey makes some of the very finest home made wines. And what is more, it is one of the easiest of wines to make successfully.

Mead is obtainable from commercial producers at prices ranging from 8/6 to 12/6 per bottle. Making mead is a good deal cheaper than this. Details for making this should be included in this book if only because this book deals with making wines from readily obtainable ingredients. But this is not possible for I have included fully-detailed mead-making in *Home Brewing Without Failures*, which also includes the making of cider, ales, beers, stouts and lager.

25

Inexpensive Liqueurs

There is no doubt that the taste for liqueurs is taking hold of a great many people – regardless of their cost. Taking a liqueur over the bar is one thing, but making a bottle of it is something totally different, as is buying a bottle.

Buying bottles of liqueurs – even if you have a 'thing' about them – can prove nigh-on prohibitive for ordinary folk, yet it is the ordinary folk who are now getting the taste for them.

This chapter is designed to show how you can make at a great saving some very excellent liqueurs from wines made from T'Noirot extract.

In these we have the flavour of many liqueurs, and since we have made at very little cost 14% of the alcohol needed, the rest is comparatively simple.

The alcohol content of liqueurs varies a good deal. For example, most cherry brandies are about 40% proof, while other liqueurs may be in the region of 75-80 or even 90% proof. There seems to be some misunderstanding in the difference between proof and the actual alcohol content which is better understood if referred to as alcohol by

156

volume. Many people are puzzled when they read of being able to obtain spirit of 140% or 158% proof. They are puzzled as to how it is possible to obtain higher than 100%.

The use of 'proof' is a relic of the past. A spirit of 140% proof has an alcohol content 80% by volume, while a spirit of 158% proof is 90%.

It is the alcohol by volume we shall concern ourselves with here and the table on this page shows the relation between alcohol by volume and proof spirit.

Therefore we can see the percent proof obtained by making a liqueur of a certain percentage of alcohol by volume.

ALCOHOL TABLE

Alcohol percent by Volume	*Per cent proof*	
50	87·6	
45	78·8	
40	70	Gin
35	61·2	
30	52·4	
25	43·8	
20	35	
19	33·1	} Vermouth
18	31·4	
17	29·7	
16	28	
15	26·2	
14	24·5	home-made wine

The words 'gin', 'Vermouth' and 'Home-made wine' on the right give you an idea of the difference in the strengths of various popular wines and spirits.

To make wines into liqueurs of the correct strength would be very expensive, except perhaps in the case of cherry brandy. So, provided you are prepared to have home-made liqueurs a bit lower in alcohol content than their commercial brothers you have no need to break the bank. After all, you will not be making gallons at a time, but merely a bottle now and again.

There is no point in giving here the true alcohol content of all liqueurs, because there is no need to go above the alcohol content of gin which is 40% by volume (70% proof), though, as I have said, some liqueurs are as high as 50% by volume (nearly 90% proof).

In the tables on pages 163-6 will be seen the amount of alcohol needed to raise wine of 14% by volume to whatever figure by volume you wish to achieve. Now, the first step in making wine into a liqueur is to sweeten it. And the amount of sugar to add will depend on personal taste and whether the wine is dry, medium or sweet. To sweeten you merely add sugar, but to add this to cold wine would mean hours of stirring to dissolve it.

Therefore, take half of a bottle of wine and put this into a polythene or china jug. Stand this in a saucepan of water over heat so that it gets warm but not hot. Keep the wine covered. Put in two or three teaspoonfuls of sugar and stir when the wine is warm. Repeat until sugar is dissolved keeping wine covered with, say, a saucer. When all sugar is dissolved, using a funnel, return the sweetened wine to the bottle and sample. If this is sweet enough, this is all that is needed. On the other hand if more sugar is needed the process may be repeated. If too much sugar has been added, some of the same batch of wine can be mixed with the over-sweetened bottle.

When you have the bottle of wine sweetened to taste you may consult the Liqueur Table on page 163 in order to find how much alcohol to add to give you the percentage of alcohol by volume you want to increase to. And if you want to know the percentage of proof spirit this will contain you merely check with the Alcohol Table on page ooo.

ALCOHOL BY VOLUME PERCENT

This means the percentage of alcohol by volume. For example, for the purpose of finding the percentage of alcohol in a bottle of wine it must be regarded as having 100 volumes. Therefore a bottle of wine of fourteen percent of alcohol by volume contains fourteen parts of pure alcohol per one hundred parts. To make it simpler, if we could divide a bottle of wine into one hundred parts, the alcohol if separated would form fourteen parts of the one hundred parts.

DIFFERENCES IN BOTTLE SIZES

An important point to bear in mind when making up these liqueurs is the different sizes of bottles used for keeping wines. The standard British wine bottle in which most wines are sold and in which gin and whisky are sold hold 26 and $\frac{2}{3}$ fluid ounces. Filled to the usual level the contents amount to 26 oz. But many bottles of imported wines, those decorative sorts and those with no shoulders like the British standard wine bottle has, hold about one pint, but sometimes a little more. Therefore, it would be worth while investing in a fluid ounce measure. These are quite cheap.

SWEETENING

If you are going to increase the alcohol to a high percentage it will be seen that the amount of alcohol needed will reduce the sweetness to some extent, so it would be wise to sweeten more than you need in this case rather than having to sweeten further after the alcohol has been added.

STRENGTH OF FLAVOUR

Where relatively small amounts of alcohol are added the strength of flavour of the wine made into liqueurs will not be weakened to any great extent. But where goodly amounts are added, the flavour will, of course be reduced. This need not dismay you. All you need to do to rectify matters is to add – drop at a time – some of the extract used to flavour the wine. If you have to do this, use an eye-dropper or a pippette, if you have such a thing. Bear in mind that very little extract will be needed owing to its concentrated strength of flavour.

Adding sugar to the wine to sweeten will reduce the alcohol just a little, but this may be ignored. The figures given in the liqueur tables do not take into account this slight reduction.

The whole idea behind using Vodka or Polish spirit is so that we can increase the alcohol without affecting the colour or flavour. Brandy or whisky would ruin these wines because of their flavours. Both the spirits mentioned have neither colour nor flavour.

I have not included a table for using spirit of 158% proof because this is not now readily obtainable.

TABLES 1 AND 2

Where Vodka is used it will be seen that the tables (1 and 2) do not go higher than 27% by volume (46% proof). This is because to go higher using Vodka the dilution of the flavour of the wine might be too great. Therefore, if you want to go above this figure it would be best to use Polish pure spirit and tables 3 and 4 (see Appendix for address of supplier of Polish pure spirit).

Liqueur Table No. 1

Using Vodka to make 20 oz. (1 pint)

Add these fl. oz. Vodka of 70% proof (40% by volume) to	*these fl. oz. of sweetened wine of 14% by volume*	*to obtain 1 pint liqueur containing this percent of alcohol by volume*
1	19	15·3
2	18	16·6
3	17	17·9
4	16	19·2
5	15	20·5
6	14	21·8
7	13	23·1
8	12	24·4
9	11	25·7
10	10	27·0

See Alcohol Table to find percent proof of the liqueurs containing the percent of alcohol by volume to which you have increased.

LIQUEUR TABLE NO. 2

Using Vodka to make 26 fl. oz.
(1 standard wine bottle)

Add these fl. oz. Vodka of 70% proof (40% by volume) to	*these fl. oz. of sweetened wine of 14% by volume*	*to **obtain** 26 fl. oz. liqueur containing this percent of alcohol by volume*
1	25	15
2	24	16
3	23	17
4	22	18
5	21	19
6	20	20
7	19	21
8	18	22
9	17	23
10	16	24
11	15	25
12	14	26
13	13	27

Using Polish pure spirit to make 20 fl. oz. (1 pint)
See Alcohol Table to find percent proof of the liqueurs containing the percent of alcohol by volume to which you have increased.

Liqueur Table No. 3

Add these fl. oz. of Polish pure spirit of 140% proof (80% by volume) to	these fl. oz. of sweetened wine of 14% by volume	to obtain 1 pint liqueur containing this percent of alcohol by volume
1	19	17·3
2	18	20·6
3	17	23·9
4	16	27·2
5	15	30·5
6	14	33·8
7	13	37·1
8	12	40·4
9	11	43·7
10	10	47·0

See Alcohol Table to find percent proof of the liqueur containing the percent of alcohol by volume to which you have increased.

LIQUEUR TABLE NO. 4

Using Polish pure spirit to make 26 fl. oz.
(1 standard wine bottle)

Add these fl. oz. of Polish pure spirit of 140% proof (80% by volume) to	these fl. oz. of sweetened wine of 14% by volume	to obtain 26 fl. oz. liqueur containing this percent of alcohol by volume
1	25	16·5
2	24	19·1
3	23	21·6
4	22	24·2
5	21	26·7
6	20	29·2
7	19	31·8
8	18	34·3
9	17	36·8
10	16	39·4
11	15	41·9
12	14	44·5
13	13	47·0

See Alcohol Table to find the percent proof of the liqueur containing the percent of alcohol by volume to which you have increased.

As already mentioned, there is no need to go higher than 70% proof (40% by volume). This is a very high percentage of alcohol and while, as we have already seen, some liqueurs are as high as 90% proof, many are a good deal lower than 70% proof. All in all, I would say that to fortify to between 18% and 30% by volume for general purposes would be sufficient with perhaps going as high as 40% by volume in rare cases.

If you merely want to fortify unsweetened wine to be used as wines for ordinary purposes and not as liqueurs, 1, 2, or 3 fl. oz. of spirit may be used. A quick glance at the top of each liqueur table will show you what the result would be.

Liqueurs made with the highest addition of Polish pure spirit will cost about half the normal cost of commercial liqueurs. Those made with less spirit will, of course, cost a good deal less.

To Make a Trial Lot

To try our liqueur-making, you might like to make small trial lots using reduced amounts of wine and spirit, while keeping to the ratios set out in the tables.

For example you could make a quarter pint or quarter bottle according to whichever table you wish. Table 1, for example, gives at one point, 4 oz. of spirit with 16 oz. of sweetened wine. So a trial lot with this example would be 1 oz. of spirit with 4 oz. of sweetened wine. You can, of course, choose whichever ratio you wish – by this I mean set of figures across the tables.

26

Wines from Fruit Pulps

Fruit pulps are another boon to wine-makers short of garden and wild fruits. Wines made from these are really delightful, and as with other ingredients mentioned in this book, there is precious little to do by way of preparing them. Besides this, the pulps are very reasonably priced at between fifteen and seventeen shillings per tin. This size tin makes two gallons of fully-flavoured wines.

So one gallon at, say, eight shillings, results in six bottles of top-class wine of good character and bouquet at one-and-fourpence each.

When following the recipes it may be found that the resulting wine is not quite sweet enough for your liking, or perhaps it might be a little too sweet. It all depends on personal tastes.

In saying this, I do not suggest that this will be the case, I mention it as being a possibility. Either way, if the wine is just a little too sweet or a little too dry the fault – if you can call it that – is simplicity itself to remedy. How to do this is covered in earlier chapters.

I found it best when using pulps for the first time

167

to make single gallon lots and to blend them if necessary (see Blending p. 65). I have used the hydrometer to obtain special results, but you will have no real need for it here unless you happen to have been making wines for some time and use it habitually, when you will, of course, use it as a matter of course.

I used to use all sorts of apparatus including the hydrometer for almost all my wine-making, but I have found that as one's experience grows the less apparatus one needs. In other words, the more experience you have, the less you will have need for anything else. Experience can come only in making wines and being observant and learning how to make them to your own particular needs and tastes.

If you have a hydrometer and want to use it with pulps, the same principle as used for concentrated grape juice may be employed. Just let me say that the pulps obtainable from different suppliers vary slightly, but this need not bother you unduly for they all may be used with the recipes here. The resulting wine will, of course, be slightly different. For this reason it is best to stick to one supplier, for you will then know in advance that the result will be to your liking.

The pulps available are apricot, pineapple and peach.

RECIPE

Tin of fruit pulp of your choice · 5¼ lb. sugar
½ oz. citric or tartaric acid · ½ cupful strong, freshly
made tea · All-purpose wine yeast · nutrient and
water as in method

Put pulp in saucepan with equal quantity of water. Bring just to boiling point and pour into fermenting vessel. Boil 5 lbs. sugar for two minutes in one gallon water (or make two half-gallon lots of it if more convenient), and pour into pulp. Allow to cool, add tea, acid, yeast and nutrient. Cover as directed and ferment for ten days. Then put as near half in two separate one-gallon jars. Fill one to where neck begins with boiled cooled water.

To the second jar add one pint of water in which the remaining $\frac{1}{4}$ lb. of sugar has been boiled and allowed to cool. Then fill to where neck begins with boiled cooled water.

Fit fermentation lock to each and leave until all fermentation has ceased.

The above will give you two separate gallons – one very slightly sweeter than the other. Both may be exactly what you want, if they are not, they may be blended together or the one may be left dry and the other sweetened a little more. It is all a matter of taste.

I have found that the apricot wine is ready to drink in as little as seven-eight months. The others need longer to mellow down.

27

Some Questions and Answers

Q. All my utensils being on the large size I find it more convenient to make all my wines in four-gallon lots. But I do not want to do this with T'Noirot extract wines.

What I want is your opinion on this. Suppose I make a four-gallon lot of parsnip or some other wine suitable as a basic wine for use with the extracts and then, when it would normally be put into a four-gallon jar, divide it into four separate one-gallon lots and put the required amount of different extract into each gallon. If I do this, surely I would obtain four gallons of different wines from the original four-gallon lot?

A. Of course you would. Excellent idea this. You would, of course, have to add the final sugar addition before dividing the brew. Having done this, divide it, add the extract of your choice to each gallon and then ferment on to completion regarding each as a separate batch.

Anyone making wines on a large scale could do the same. Make, say, ten gallons; six to be made into T'Noirot wines of their choice and the remainder fermented on parsnip wine as in the case of my correspondent.

Q. I have been given two old vinegar barrels and would like you to tell me what I ought to do to make them suitable for storing wines.

A. The only thing to do with those barrels is to burn them. On second thoughts, you could use them for growing geraniums, but for heaven's sake on no account put wine into them otherwise you run the risk of all your wines turning to vinegar.

Q. I have five gallons of wine made from the Dold synthetic Must. This is light and dry and I like to take a little before my evening meal. But five gallons is a lot especially as I have another five gallons almost ready for bottling. What I would like to do is to flavour two or three separate gallons with different T'Noirot extracts, but I must be sure I would obtain what I am after – that is a good wine with a good all-round flavour and bouquet.

A. If your synthetic Must wine is in itself a good all-round wine there is no reason at all why it should not be improved by flavouring it. Any of the extracts would go well with the finished wine and because so little extract is needed to flavour a gallon, you would not be reducing the alcohol content to any noticeable extent. But if you want to make up for the dilution an ounce or two of Vodka per gallon would do the trick.

HYDROMETER PUZZLE

Q. I am using two hydrometers for finding the sugar content of concentrated grape juice. I use one reading from 1·100 to 1·200 to find the sugar content when the juice is diluted to half the full extent so that I know how much sugar to add before diluting to the full. In most cases I get a first reading of 1·180. From this I calculate that when diluted to the full I shall have a reading of 1·090. But I do not get this reading. The hydrometers I have are rather old. Could you give me an explanation for the apparent mystery?

A. It would appear from what you tell me that the hydrometer you are using for your second test, the one reading from 1·000 to 1·100, is inaccurate. If it were not, you would obtain a reading when the juice is diluted to the full of the figure you quote – that is 1·090.

You say your hydrometers are rather old and it could be that there is a slight crack in the one in question. And since some of the older hydrometers are hollow in places it could be that a little water has got into it.

To test for this, fill the sample glass with water and put the hydrometer into this. If there is a fault it will be noticeable at once because a hydrometer reading from 1·000 to 1·100 should float so that the water cuts across the stem at the figure of 1·000, this figure being the gravity of water. But if it is heavier than it should be, owing to the reason suggested or for a fault in the manufacture, it will sink lower and so give a lower reading.

Q. May I use concentrated grape juice with T'Noirot extracts? I have the feeling that if I use white concentrate for say, Vermouth, I would have the genuine stuff as against an imitation as when this is made with potatoes and such like.

A. You may be right about having the genuine

stuff when using grape juice, but this would make the wine rather expensive. The fact that when potatoes or other cheap ingredients are used we get an imitation does not really matter because the imitation is so much like the genuine article as to be almost identical – except, of course, to the connoisseur.

Q. I have twenty-five gallons of rhubarb wine, and I fear that before I have used all this for what it is it will lose its quality. After all, this being more of an aperitif rather than a wine for evening use, I take just a little with my evening meal.

As this will last a great length of time, and because I can make much more any time I am wondering whether I could flavour a few gallons of this with T'Noirot extract.

A. Almost all the flavour in rhubarb wine comes from the oxalic acid present so if you remove the acid in a few gallons you would have a wine of practically no flavour quite suitable for use with T'Noirot extracts.

Having removed the acid in the following manner all that would be needed would be the addition of sufficient extract of your choice – about 2 fl. oz. per gallon. But you would have to add a little acid to the wine otherwise it would lack bite. This could be done by adding a $\frac{1}{4}$ oz. of citric acid from a chemist or by adding the strained juice of two lemons.

Put one gallon of rhubarb wine into a polythene pail. Take about half a pint of this. Into this half-pint stir one ounce of precipitated chalk from a chemist (about 3d.). When this is dissolved, stir it into the bulk. Some frothing will occur. Cover and leave for about an hour. Then siphon the clear wine off the chalk deposit but not until it is quite clear.

This will have practically no flavour because the chalk will have crystalised the acid which is now settled to the bottom with the chalk. So you may add the extract of your choice and if you like an ounce of Vodka per bottle – 6 per gallon – to make up for the dilution.

The citric acid may be added at the same time as the extract. But do not add anything until the wine is brilliantly clear.

Appendix

The following is a list of suppliers of ingredients and utensils mentioned in this book. Beside each is stated the nature of their supplies.

Fermenta, 59-60, Kingston Rd., New Malden, Surrey — Yeasts, nutrients, T'Noirot extracts

Semplex, Old Hall Works, Stuart Rd., Higher Tranmere, Birkenhead, Cheshire — All utensils, yeasts, nutrients, dried fruits, pulps and concentrates

Joseph Bryant Ltd., 95 Old Market St., Bristol 2 — All utensils, corks, bungs, jars, etc.

Winemaker's Equipment Ltd., 242 Deansgate, Manchester 3 — All requirements

Home Winemakers Supplies Co., 6 Withy Grove, Manchester 4 — All requirements

Leigh, Williams and Sons, 9 Easter Drive, Grassendale, Liverpool 19 — All requirements

Southern Vineyards, 26 Conway St., Hove, Sussex — Yeasts, nutrients and grape juice

W. R. Loftus, 24 Tottenham Court Rd., London W.1 — All requirements

M. Agusti Hidalgo, 81 Ledbury Rd., London, W. 11 — Grape juices and fruit pulps

In Canada
Wine Art, P/O Box 2701, Vancouver 3, B.C. — All requirements and utensils
  Also serves large areas of U.S.A.

In U.S.A.
Aetna Bottle Co. Inc., 708 Rainier Avenue South, Seattle, 44 Washington — All needs and utensils

In New Zealand
Brewers Trading Co., P/O Box 593, Christchurch, New Zealand — All ingredients and utensils. Also serves Australia

Polish Pure spirit for fortifying or liqueur-making may be obtained from Turner Roche & Co. Ltd., 21, Old Compton St., London W.1., and is sometimes obtainable from wine merchants.